Scriptwriting

UEA Scriptwriting 2012

First published by Egg Box Publishing 2012
International © retained by individual authors

This book is sold subject to the condition that it shall not, by way of trade or otherwise, be lent, resold, hired out, stored in a retrieval system, or otherwise circulated without the publisher's prior consent in any form of binding or cover other than that in which it is published and without a similar condition including this condition being imposed on the subsequent purchaser.

A CIP record for this book is available from the British Library.

UEA Scriptwriting 2012 is typeset in Caslon 10pt on 13pt leading with Din titles.

Printed and bound in the UK by CPI Antony Rowe Ltd.

Designed and typeset by Sean Purdy at The Ampersand.
Cover photography by Jerusha Green.

Proofread by Sarah Gooderson

Distributed by Central Books

ISBN: 9780956928955

UEA Anthology 2012

Acknowledgments

Thanks to the following for making this anthology possible:

The Malcolm Bradbury Memorial Fund, the Centre for Creative and Performing Arts at the University of East Anglia and The School of Literature, Drama and Creative Writing at UEA in partnership with Egg Box Publishing.

We'd also like to thank the following people:

Moniza Alvi, Jean Boase-Beier, Amit Chaudhuri, Andrew Cowan, William Fiennes, Giles Foden, Sarah Gooderson, Lavinia Greenlaw, Rachel Hore, Kathryn Hughes, Katie Konyn, Michael Lengsfield, Jean McNeil, Natalie Mitchell, Jeremy Page, Rob Ritchie, Helen Smith, Henry Sutton, George Szirtes, Val Taylor and Steve Waters.
Nathan Hamilton at Egg Box Publishing, Sean Purdy and Jerusha Green.

Editorial team:
Linda Black
Natasha Broad
Gaynor Clements
Ella Chappell
Eluned Gramich
Tilly Lunken
Erin Meier
Judy O'Kane

Contents

Foreword
Val Taylor — *1*

Contributors
Linda C Black — *8*
Rick Blakely — *22*
Mark Boutros — *30*
Shorelle Cole — *48*
Beth Crane — *58*
Georgina Kuna — *62*
Tilly Lunken — *78*
Waleed Marzouk — *90*
Oliver Michell — *106*
Andy Moseley — *116*

Interview
Steve Waters — *130*

UEA Anthology 2012

Foreword

by Val Taylor

Linda C Black
Rick Blakely
Mark Boutros
Shorelle Cole
Beth Crane
Georgina Kuna
Tilly Lunken
Waleed Marzouk
Oliver Michell
Andy Moseley

In Luigi Pirandello's *Six Characters in Search of an Author* (1921), the Father – a troubled philosopher – claims that the Characters are more 'real' than the actors whose play rehearsal they have gatecrashed. He argues that the (fictive) Characters are immutable, their orbits fixed; whereas the actors (as living people) remake themselves, and are remade, moment by moment, in the act of living. The Characters have one story, within which each Character's identity is precisely prescribed. The actors have no fixed orbit, no single story – perhaps, no story at all.

Playwright Michelene Wandor, in *The Art of Writing Drama* (2008), describes 'character' as 'a can of worms'. Drama is not, she argues, 'about' character; its function is not to unpack individual biographies, but to animate relationships between characters in context. The identity of Pirandello's Characters has been forged – and fixed – through their web of inter-relationships. Wandor would, perhaps, reclaim the capacity for characters to make and remake themselves through interaction, but both writers, it seems, agree on the dramatic significance of relationships between characters.

It strikes me that 'a can of worms' would be an apposite description of the relationships between Pirandello's Six Characters. And perhaps each Character is, him- or herself, also a 'can of worms': a tangled mass of secrets, lies and truths, bravery and cowardice, love and disgust, beauty and ugliness. When the Six Characters interact, those hidden contradictions are opened to our view.

Following in the footsteps of Pirandello and Wandor, we might look forward, in this volume of the 2012 Anthology, to judicious prisings-open of tightly-sealed cans and the discovery of worms therein, as this year's Scriptwriting MA authors introduce their characters to one another, and to us.

....

Val Taylor is Director of Scriptwriting at UEA.

by Val Taylor

Linda C Black

Bye-Bye Beautiful
A Short Film

FADE IN:

EXT. SCHOOL – DAY

A jeep parks outside the school. Notes of a nursery song, *Baa Baa Black Sheep,* begin to play.

NATASHA, 6, jumps down from the high jeep. She has been smoothed over, but her scruffy nature wins.

          NATASHA'S MUM (OS)
        Bye-bye, beautiful.

Natasha sings *Baa Baa Black Sheep* as she plods across the playground and joins a group of kids.

All put a foot in the middle. JACK taps their feet. Natasha continues to sing. She speaks in rhythm to her tune.

              JACK
        Eeny, meany, miny, mo. Catch a
        tiger by the toe. If he screams, let
        him go …

            NATASHA
        Mum says I cannot sleep at yours.

                        JACK
                Eeny, meany ...

                        SALLY
                Aw!

                        JACK
                Miny, mo. Sally, you're it.

SALLY folds her arms and turns to Natasha.

                        SALLY
                No! Come on Natasha, let's go.

Sally pulls Natasha away. They walk into the building. A chubby boy, DAN, follows them.

INT. CORRIDOR – DAY

Natasha hums her tune now, as she, Sally and Dan walk down the colourful corridor.

                    DAN (SINGS)
                Yes sir, yes sir—

Natasha glares at Dan. He stops singing. Natasha and Sally enter the girls' bathroom. Dan waits outside.

                    DAN (SINGS)
                Three bags full.

INT. BATHROOM – DAY

Natasha, still humming, and Sally enter and lock their separate cubicles.

by Linda C Black

Their feet dangle under the door as trickles tinkle for a moment.

INT. CLASSROOM – DAY

MISS HOOPER sits at the front of the class. We never see above her waist.

Natasha plays with the tune in her breath and nods her head to it. She sits beside Jack, who is turned around to show the BOY behind him a frog in his hand.

> **MISS HOOPER**
> Jack.

> **JACK**
> School dinner, Miss.

Natasha peers over her desk to see Jack's hand. This stops her song.

> **MISS HOOPER**
> Dan.

> **DAN**
> Pack lunch, Miss.

> **MISS HOOPER**
> Natasha.

Natasha is still engrossed with the boys' hands. Miss Hooper puts her pen down. She stands and walks to the boys.

> **MISS HOOPER (CONT'D)**
> Boys?

Jack looks up and quickly dashes his hand under the desk.

JACK
Yes, Miss Hooper?

Miss Hooper holds her hand out and waits with her hand on her hip. Jack presents the frog to her. She takes it and drops it out the window. Sally holds her hand up.

MISS HOOPER
Yes, Sally? Is it quick?

SALLY
What are we doing today, Miss?

Natasha starts to hum again at *One for my master*.

MISS HOOPER
Today we have numeracy after break. Natasha.

Natasha looks up at Miss Hooper. She stops her hum.

MISS HOOPER (CONT'D)
After lunch we will learn about bodies, and now, I want you all to go to the carpet for reading.

Miss Hooper claps her hands. The class clambers to the carpet and fights for spots.

Natasha takes her time as she dances in time to the song in her head.

INT. CLASSROOM – DAY

Miss Hooper reads from a book as the class sits on the floor. Natasha pays close attention. Dan watches Sally.

by Linda C Black

> **MISS HOOPER**
> She was the most beautiful girl he had ever seen.

Miss Hooper lowers the book.

> **MISS HOOPER (CONT'D)**
> What words did he use to tell us that she is beautiful?

Little hands dart up.

> **MISS HOOPER (CONT'D)**
> Jane?

> **JANE**
> Golden hair.

> **MISS HOOPER**
> Yes. And why does that mean beautiful?

Hands go down.

> **MISS HOOPER (CONT'D)**
> Gold is a precious metal, isn't it? It makes you think of something expensive and special. What else?

Hands go up.

> **MISS HOOPER (CONT'D)**
> Sally?

SALLY
Rosy cheeks and perfect lips.

Hands go down.

MISS HOOPER
Yes, that's all the rest, thank you Sally. Remember to let others answer too.

Natasha puts up her hand.

MISS HOOPER (CONT'D)
Yes, Natasha?

NATASHA
What does it mean if you don't have golden hair, rosy cheeks and perfect lips?

JACK
That you're ugly!

The class laughs.

MISS HOOPER
Jack!

JACK
The opposite of beautiful is ugly, so if you're not beautiful, you're ugly.

NATASHA
Well, I must be ugly, then.

by Linda C Black

The class laughs.

                MISS HOOPER
        That's not true. Jack, have you ever heard 'beauty is in the eye of the beholder'?

Jack shakes his head.

             MISS HOOPER (CONT'D)
        That means that each person can see beauty in a different way. For the boy in the book, these things were beautiful, but that doesn't mean that someone else thought the same. Natasha, you're not ugly.

Natasha considers this, unconvinced.

EXT. PLAYGROUND – DAY

Natasha dances down a hopscotch mark-out as she sings *Hey Diddle Diddle* in full volume.

Sally huffs beside it and Dan stands a little to the side.

                   SALLY
        You're not doing it right!

Sally picks up a pebble and passes it to Natasha.

                    DAN
        Why are you singing that song?

                    SALLY
        Dan, go away!

Dan shuffles back a step. Natasha lowers to a hum. She takes the pebble and throws it at the beginning.

DAN
Sally, what are we doing after lunch?

Natasha skips down the hopscotch. She speaks in rhythm to her song.

NATASHA
We're going to the computers.

SALLY
No, we're learning about bodies. Miss Hooper said so. That's not right!

Sally moves Natasha off the markings and demonstrates how to play. Natasha stops her song.

NATASHA
What about bodies?

DAN
How they work?

SALLY
Miss Hooper said last week that we'd talk about boys and girls. I asked her after class. Then we're doing men and women.

by Linda C Black

NATASHA

That's easy. Boys wear trousers. Girls wear skirts. Boys like sport, girls like … pink.

Natasha shrugs at them. Dan and Sally shake their heads.

DAN

I like pink.

SALLY

Go away, Dan!

NATASHA

Well, boys have short hair and girls have long hair.

Natasha looks at them to see if she is right this time. Dan chooses his words carefully.

DAN

Boys can pee standing up.

NATASHA

So can I.

SALLY

Can you?

Natasha ponderously nods and begins to hum *Ring A Ring A Rosie* as she starts to skip on the markings.

SALLY (CONT'D)

I want to try.

Sally grabs Natasha's hand and pulls her into the school. Dan watches them curiously, then potters along behind them.

INT. BATHROOM – DAY

Sally pulls Natasha, who hums *Ring A Ring A Rosie*, into the room.

They each go into a cubicle and lock the doors. Their feet face the toilets.

      SALLY
  Are you doing it?

Natasha stops humming.

      NATASHA
  Not yet.

      SALLY
  Together.

A splash from Natasha's cubicle echoes on the toilet bowl while a splash from Sally's hits the floor. She giggles.

     SALLY (CONT'D)
  Ah!

Sally's feet turn and dangle under the cubicle.

     SALLY (CONT'D)
  Did you do it?

INT. CLASSROOM – DAY

The children whisper to each other as Miss Hooper types. Natasha hums *Baa Baa Black Sheep* again and watches the girl in front draw flowers.

by Linda C Black

Miss Hooper stands up. Natasha stops humming and puts her hand up.

> **MISS HOOPER**
> Right. Oh, Natasha, is it about our topic?

Natasha nods.

> **MISS HOOPER (CONT'D)**
> All right then.

> **NATASHA**
> Is it OK if a girl isn't like other girls? Is she still a girl?

> **MISS HOOPER**
> What do you mean, Natasha?

> **NATASHA**
> I'm a girl. But I don't like what other girls like. I don't like wearing skirts. Or drawing flowers. Or pink. And I can pee standing up, but other girls can't.

The class laughs. Miss Hooper places her hand on her hips. They settle, as they stare up in fear of her teacher stare, but are on the verge of laughing again.

> **MISS HOOPER**
> Natasha. What you do or don't like doesn't make you a boy or a girl. It's about your body.

Jack's hand shoots up.

> **MISS HOOPER (CONT'D)**
> Yes, Jack?

> **JACK**
> Boys have penises and girls have vaginas.

Laughter erupts from the children. Miss Hooper suppresses her own laughter as she settles them.

> **MISS HOOPER**
> Yes, Jack, that's right.

Miss Hooper hits a button on her computer and two bodies appear on the smartboard, anatomically correct. The class laughs.

> **MISS HOOPER (CONT'D)**
> All right, all right.

Natasha puts her hand up.

> **MISS HOOPER (CONT'D)**
> Yes, Natasha.

> **NATASHA**
> Why does the boy have long hair and the girl have short hair? You said it was about their bodies.

Miss Hooper turns to the board. Then to Natasha.

> **MISS HOOPER**
> Ah, no, Natasha.

by Linda C Black

Miss Hooper walks up to the board and labels the boy and girl. The children giggle as she does this, but Natasha concentrates on the board.

Miss Hooper turns to the class when they are loud and they react to her teacher stare again. As she finishes, Miss Hooper turns to Natasha.

> **MISS HOOPER (CONT'D)**
> That better?

Natasha considers the board. Concentration spreads through the class as they all notice Miss Hooper focused on her.

> **MISS HOOPER (CONT'D)**
> Natasha?

> **NATASHA**
> Well, I'm a boy then.

The class erupts. Miss Hooper is taken aback, but quickly gets to work settling the class down from this.

> **MISS HOOPER**
> Ah, quiet, please. Jack! Sit down.
> Class two; I am not impressed, you
> should know better. Now, settle
> down.

Natasha sits still and considers in the middle of chaos.

EXT. SCHOOL – DAY

The jeep parks outside the school. Natasha, now with short hair, jumps nonchalantly out of the jeep in trousers.

NATASHA'S MUM
Bye-bye, beau—

The car door shuts and cuts off Natasha's Mum's sniffle.

    Natasha starts to sing *Baa Baa*
    Black Sheep and plods through the
    playground.

THE END

....

Linda C Black has lived in Northern Ireland, America, Belgium and the fine city of Norwich, which would account for her strange accent and quirky ideas. She writes about all of this, and more, in her blog *Elsie B Writes*.

by Linda C Black

Rick Blakely

Guests For Dinner
A Short Film

INT. DINING/LIVING ROOM, ERIC'S FLAT – DAY

Metal clinks of the lock being picked from outside. The front door is slowly pushed open. JAMES (29) and HARRY (26) step inside carrying empty backpacks. They glance around.

In front of them a round dining table covered with papers. A hatch between this room and the kitchen. A chair sits out from the table. A scuffmark on the floor.

Clean shirts hang over an armchair, which has been knocked askew. Two matching sofas and another armchair sit around a glass coffee table.

Along one wall is a bookcase, half the shelves taken up by cookbooks. In the middle of the bookcase a Bose sound system. On top a number of South Pacific trinkets, complementing the tapestries decorating the walls.

Harry sweeps the trinkets into his bag.

James flicks through the human anatomy essays and diagrams on the table. He quickly loses interest.

INT. DINING/LIVING ROOM, ERIC'S FLAT – DAY

James examines the Bose system. Harry joins him.

HARRY
Nice piece of equipment. What is it?

JAMES
It's a Bose Lifestyle V-Class Entertainment System.

James unplugs the cables from the back.

JAMES (CONT'D)
Go get the speakers.

Harry moves away. James loads the main piece of the sound system into his backpack with the cables on top.

Harry returns, mission accomplished.

JAMES (CONT'D)
Let's see what he's got in his bedroom.

Harry follows James into the bedroom.

INT. BEDROOM, ERIC'S FLAT – DAY

There are wrinkles on the otherwise neatly made bed. The rug at the foot of the bed is slightly underneath.

Harry examines a pile of old clothes on the floor next to the bathroom door, a pair of well-worn muddy boots resting on top. He lifts up a ragged, heavily patched shirt.

James opens the wardrobe. Extracts some expensive shirts.

              JAMES
    Here, Harry. Give us your bag.

Harry glances up.

           JAMES (CONT'D)
    Why are you bothering with that
    crap when he's got stuff like this?

James sets a £165 Dolce & Gabbana shirt on the bed.

Harry holds the old shirt in one hand. Passes the bag with the other. The trinkets clink.

             HARRY
    Why would a man who can afford
    hundred-pound shirts and expensive
    speaker systems keep shit clothes
    like this?

James empties the bag.

             JAMES
    Maybe he has an allotment. You
    don't think he'd be wearing shirts
    like these for that do you?

James lines the bag with neatly folded shirts.

             HARRY
    No. But he could at least have better

gardening clothes than this.

James replaces the trinkets and speakers, padded with shirts.

                  JAMES
        Maybe they hold sentimental value.

James hands the bag back. Walks to the chest of drawers.

Harry goes to get the laptop sitting on the desk in the corner. His bag is too full to accommodate it.

Harry glances at the corkboard on the wall. Bills, reminders, a photograph of Eric's parents, and newspaper clippings of missing persons. James's voice snaps him out of his examination. The laptop is still in his hand.

              JAMES (CONT'D)
        Why don't you make yourself useful?

Harry looks round. James stands by the open top drawer.

              JAMES (CONT'D)
        Pass me that Kindle.

Harry reaches across the bed. Grabs the Kindle. Takes it and the laptop to James, who inserts them into his own bag.

              JAMES (CONT'D)
        See what's in the bathroom.

INT. BATHROOM, ERIC'S FLAT – DAY

Harry steps into the vinyl-floored bathroom. Glances around. He starts as he notices something on the handle at the side of the bathtub.

He looks closer. A fingerprint in dried blood.

Harry steps back. He goes to the cabinet over the sink. Opens it. Casts a cursory glance over the contents. Closes the cabinet door.

INT. BEDROOM, ERIC'S FLAT – DAY

James extracts an expensive watch and a pair of cufflinks from the top drawer as Harry steps out of the bathroom.

> **JAMES**
> Well? Anything?

> **HARRY**
> Um.
> (A beat)
> No. Shall I check out the kitchen?

> **JAMES**
> You're an idiot. What are you going to find in the kitchen?

> **HARRY**
> He might have silver cutlery.

> **JAMES**
> Fine. I'll be right out.

Harry goes out with his bag. James opens each drawer. Fishes around. Everything is neatly organised and folded. No hidden treasures. James picks up his backpack. Follows Harry.

INT. KITCHEN, ERIC'S FLAT – DAY

The kitchen sports marble counters along three sides. A window looks out to the street. Dishes sit in the sink and drying rack.

Harry goes straight to the fridge by the utility room door. Looks inside. On the top shelf are three raw steaks on a plate covered in clingfilm. There are also leftovers, sauces, milk, eggs, and vegetables.

The fridge door is still open when James enters.

          JAMES
     This is no time to be eating. I
     thought you were checking out the
     cutlery drawers.

          HARRY
     Yes. I was. I—

          JAMES
     I'll do it.

James points at the utility room door.

          JAMES
     See what's through there.

Harry closes the door. Goes into the utility room. James opens the first drawer.

In the utility room, Harry can be heard opening cupboard doors and drawers. He opens a waist-high freezer. Drops it closed.

          HARRY (OS)
     J-James.

by Rick Blakely

James looks round.

                    JAMES
          What?

                HARRY (OS)
        I think you'd better see this.

James goes into the utility room.

INT. UTILITY ROOM, ERIC'S FLAT – DAY

Harry stands in front of the freezer. James joins him. He lifts the lid. Glances inside. Immediately drops it closed.

                    HARRY
       I think we'd better get out of here.

INT. DINING/LIVING ROOM, ERIC'S FLAT – DAY

James and Harry freeze as the door handle turns.

The door opens. ERIC (29) stands in the doorway. Dressed in a smart suit, a small backpack over one shoulder, a jacket over the other. He steps inside. Closes the door behind him. Lays his jacket on the armchair. Reaches into an inside jacket pocket.

                    ERIC
       You know, I really don't like
       uninvited guests.

THE END

Rick Blakely's exhilarating childhood stemmed from having parents from different countries who brought him up in a third. Life in England is comparatively dull, and the most excitement he encounters happens to the characters in the stories he writes.

by Rick Blakely

Mark Boutros

The Man with Two Right Hands
A Webisode

EXT. STREETS – DAY

Sad music.

Run-down buildings, semi-empty, littered streets, and an empty city centre.

INT. GARY'S HOUSE – DAY

A man's right hand opens a fridge, then opens a bottle of beer.

> **GARY (VO)**
> My name is Gary Butcher, and this is my home. Beautiful Wigan. These are the shops I shop at. The streets I walk down everyday, and the place I sleep. It may all look ordinary. But my life is far from ordinary. Because I have ...

INT. GARY'S LIVING ROOM – DAY

GARY (36), ginger, unhygienic, is on the sofa. Both his hands are right hands.

> **GARY**
> ... Two right hands. I was just born like this. It's pretty annoying really. Especially at parties when the DJ says 'Everybody clap your hands' I want him to know I'm not being rude, it just looks weird like I'm takin' the piss ...

Gary lifts his hands up.

INT. GARY'S BEDROOM – DAY

Gary is watching what we've just seen, on his computer. He's wearing the same clothes.

> **GARY**
> (To camera) Not bad that Seamus? We'll have a TV deal in no time! Although, can we change the music? I want something a bit more modern. Try something by that Adele fella.

> **SEAMUS (OOV)**
> Yeah great. This camera's pretty decent ain't it?

> **GARY**
> Yeah, Shirl got it me for my thirty-sixth birthday. Makes up for that bloody skipping rope she got me last year.

An annoyed, sideways glance at SHIRLEY (36), out of Gary's league, who is stood in the doorway. She leaves, upset.

GARY (CONT'D)
(Tuts) Unbelievable.

EXT. GARY'S BALCONY – DAY

Gary is getting comfortable in his chair before addressing the camera.

GARY
Do people treat me differently? Well ... yesterday, I was wearing my favourite gilet and humming the tune to *Neighbours,* when someone called me a wanker, just coz of me 'and! The worst example was at college with the game knock down ginger.

(more)

GARY (CONT'D)
Instead of buzzing people's doors and running off, my mates used to chase me in a Fiesta. All because of this.

GARY looks at his left right hand, angrily.

GARY (CONT'D)
Ya get that bit Seamus? It's important you get the pause. It adds ... You know. It works in all them dramas, like *Supernanny.*

SEAMUS (OOV)
That ain't a drama mate.

> GARY
> What is it then?

> SEAMUS (OOV)
> Don't know, but it ain't a drama.

> GARY
> Look. You just press them buttons that make it record and don't speak anymore. You're not meant to have an identity. (Shakes Head) Did you see that bird out the window?

> SEAMUS (OOV)
> Yeah.

> GARY
> Did you film it?

> SEAMUS (OOV)
> I missed it.

> GARY
> Exactly. Because you were wafflin' about types of telly.

(more)

> GARY (CONT'D)
> We missed out on something arty. That could be the difference between a deal and a no deal. Now get back to more of this

(mimes filming)

by Mark Boutros

> **GARY (CONT'D)**
> and less of this

(mimes talking)

> You boggle my mind sometimes you do.

EXT./INT. GARY'S OFFICE – DAY

Gary enters a building. He has a huge sweat patch on the back of his shirt.

Gary's office is in the corner, away from the open plan area. People are repulsed by his BO as he passes. The bin in his office is overflowing and there are half-eaten sandwiches everywhere and empty crisp packets. It's a complete mess.

> **GARY**
> They don't want me sitting out there with the 'normals'. Probably think I'll intimidate them. I blame modern times and these 'sensitivities.' So I've got me own office.

Gary notices something moving under the mess. He stamps on it.

> **GARY (CONT'D)**
> I sometimes sit here and wonder what having two right hands would be useful for. Maybe something like holding a chainsaw. But I've never been in that situation, so I might be wrong.

INT. GARY'S LIVING ROOM – EVENING

Gary is stood with Shirley.

> **GARY**
> And they don't even make gloves for me. I always have to buy two pair. Two pair! I'm paying double to be under-advantaged!

Shirley strokes his left right hand. He looks down, inconsolable.

EXT. GARY'S FRONT DOOR – DAY – FLASHBACK

Gary is stood, staring at a handleless box. He can't lift it.

> **GARY (VO)**
> In 2001 we went through a real rough patch. While Shirl was at Tesco a box was dropped off that I couldn't move. I asked some local kids to help out but they ended up robbing everything in the house and Shirl had to move the box by herself, putting her back out ... because she's a woman.

END OF FLASHBACK

EXT. GARY'S STREET – DAY

> **GARY**
> (To Seamus) Right, we need to recreate the scene. Here, let me ask these kids.

by Mark Boutros

SEAMUS
I don't think ...

GARY
(Interrupting) Grow some doughnuts Seamus! God above.

Gary approaches some intimidating kids.

GARY (CONT'D)
Mornin' lads. Now I'm doin' a documentary about me life. And I'm doin' a reconstruction ...

HOODIE KID
(Interrupting) Is that a Blackberry?

GARY
Yes, but it's not for sale. Now let's get back to the matter at hand, excuse the pun.

HOODIE KID 2
Who said we wanted to buy it?

GARY
Great. Now come on, follow me. I'll give you some custard creams as a treat.

HOODIE KID 2
No. I mean, give us the phone.

GARY
No.

The camera shakes as Seamus slowly backs off.

> **HOODIE KID**
> Trust me. You don't want to see what's in my bag.

> **GARY**
> Is it a picture of your mum?

Gary smiles at the camera.

> **GARY (CONT'D)**
> See Seamus. (Grabbing balls) Doughnuts!

He turns back towards the kids.

Cut to:

EXT. PARK – DAY

Gary is sat on a bench. He has an eye bandage.

> **GARY**
> If I wasn't disabled, those reprobates would've felt something of a force!

Pictures flash up as he describes the different hand disguises.

> **GARY (CONT'D)**
> I've tried everything. There was the claw, which just scared people.

Gary with a claw.

> GARY (CONT'D)
> The hook, which Abu Hamza
> ruined for everyone, but now with
> this eye-bandage could be relevant
> again.

Gary with a hook.

> GARY (CONT'D)
> And finally I had this put on it ...

Gary pulls out a teddy bear that fits onto the left right hand.

> GARY (CONT'D)
> ... but people thought I was one of
> those child desirers.

EXT. STREET – DAY

Disabled people are being helped onto a bus.

> GARY (VO)
> I've decided to meet people like
> me to get an idea of how they cope
> from day to day in life.

Gary is stood among a group of people in wheelchairs, waiting to board. The CARE WORKER is ticking people off. She looks at Gary, puzzled.

> CARER
> Excuse me sir. This away day is for
> the disabled.

> **GARY**
> I am.

> **CARER**
> But ...

> **GARY**
> (Interrupting) It's fine. I'll let myself on.

Gary gets on the bus.

INT. SPECIAL BUS – DAY

Gary is talking to people.

> **FRED**
> I sometimes get people pushing me out of the way which is quite upsetting.

> **GARY**
> I hate that too. I also get people sometimes not giving up their seats for me on public transport. Do you?

> **FRED**
> (Confused) Well, no. I come with my own.

> **GARY**
> Well. I guess the Lord taketh and sometimes giveth. You should count yourself lucky.

EXT. STREET – DAY

Gary is sat on the kerb. The bus drives off.

GARY
You see. Even your own people can turn against you. I can really sympathise with Jesus.

INT. COUNCIL OFFICE – DAY

WORKER
I understand Mr Butcher. But we only assign carers to people with severe disabilities.

GARY
Are you saying? Seamus, is she saying I'm not severely disabled? I hope you're getting this. Just because I don't have a wheelychair, it doesn't make me any less disabled than a wheely. Disabled is disabled. What if those kids come back?

INT. GARY'S FLAT – DAY

Gary is on the sofa, laughing while watching TV. The door is open. BAHZNY (29, attractive, short), the carer, walks through carrying several shopping bags. He's angry.

GARY
This is Bahzny. He's me carer. Not sure about his name, but they don't exactly give you a shortlist to choose

from. (To Bahzny) Come on Bazza, these bags aren't going to empty themselves into the fridge.

Bahzny reluctantly takes the bags into the kitchen.

GARY (CONT'D)
He's all right. His heart is in the right place. He's just fucking lazy.

SEAMUS (OOV)
Why you have to swear?

GARY
Because it's gritty.

SEAMUS (OOV)
No it ain't. It's pointless. It didn't do anything.

GARY
Just shut up, all right? If you were such a pro, why has my last video only got three hits on YouTube?

SEAMUS (OOV)
Because you—

GARY
(Interrupting) I don't want you to answer that. It's so you think about it. You know, thought food. You defy boundaries sometimes, you do.

INT. OFFICE – DAY

Gary is at his desk with his feet up. Bahzny is cleaning.

> **GARY (VO)**
> He's been useful. Nobody's attacked me and he's always happy to do stuff. He's even been writing YouTube comments on my vids.

Gary hands Bahzny paperwork to do and points to the desk.

INT. GARY'S KITCHEN – NIGHT

Gary is sat at the table, alone. He can hear laughter coming from upstairs.

> **GARY**
> He goes upstairs once a day for a debrief with Shirley.

Gary sheds a single tear.

> **GARY (CONT'D)**
> We should probably sack him. I think he's stealing.

INT. GARY'S BEDROOM – DAY

Gary is sat in bed, looking devastated.

> **GARY**
> So, she's gone. Said Bahzny made her see that I've always mistreated her. Typical of a woman to be

poisoned by lies. I know it's really because he has two normal hands. Less awkward when he's playing with her nipples.

SEAMUS (OOV)
Gary. Look. You've got loads of hits!

Gary rushes to the computer. He's wearing a slanket.

GARY
I told you not to put me crying on there!

SEAMUS (OOV)
But—

GARY
No! You're a bloody idiot. You're no better than a murderer. Get out.

Gary turns the camera off.

INT. GARY'S ROOM – DAY

The camera is switched back on.

GARY
I'm sorry for blowing me top at you earlier Seamus.

SEAMUS (OOV)
That's all right.

by Mark Boutros

GARY
Good. As long as you've learned your lesson we can move on. Look at these comments.

YouTube comments:

'This man is clearly sad and deluded.' Zombiedog34

'Bellend.' Preestfaz

'I want to see more, just to feel better about my life.' KatiePrice2012

GARY (CONT'D)
We've got a following! And I know what I need to do ... win Shirl back! I'd be a hero to all those who think they're not good enough.

SEAMUS (OOV)
You going to call her and apologise?

GARY
You what? No! You don't half spout some nonsense. I'm going to set it up so she's about to get run over, then I'll jump in and save her. Like in that romantic film, *Batman*.

SEAMUS (O.O.V)
But—

GARY
(Interrupting) Don't even!

EXT. STREET – DAY

Gary is on a kerb. Shirley and Bahzny walk hand in hand in the distance.

                    GARY
           There she is with that thief.

Gary nods to someone in a car.

                GARY (CONT'D)
           That's Ramon. He says he was a
           stunt driver back in Romania.

RAMON drives towards Shirley and Bahzny. Gary starts running towards Shirley.

As the car gets close, Gary trips over, and Bahzny pushes Shirley out of the way of the car.

A crash.

INT. POLICE STATION – NIGHT

Gary is in a police station with Ramon.

                    GARY
           So, Shirley is injured in hospital,
           and Bahzny is dead. Typical of him
           to die. He struck me as weak.

Gary gives Ramon an angry look.

                GARY (CONT'D)
           You know if I had two normal hands
           I wouldn't have fallen over. It's like
           that inner ear problem, but it's inner
           hand. So unlucky.

A policeman comes to take Gary.

>   **GARY (CONT'D)**
>   The most annoying thing about it all
>   is I think I might be left-handed.

Cue sad music. Gary looks smaller as we leave the station.

THE END

Mark Boutros has worked on some of the UK's top comedy panel shows and has had written work broadcast. Being boring and useless at most things he decided to make up stories to seem more interesting. This is the best he could come up with.

by Mark Boutros

Shorelle Cole

The Babysitter's Version
A One-Act Play

Scene. A courtroom.

Five-second blackouts reflect passages of time.

Spotlight on **Losser.**

Although mid-30s, the passage of jail time and an unsettling, inhospitable childhood make convicted killer **Losser** *appear as if he's a man pushing into his 50s. He is a prominent threat by view of foot chains and jail attire, wrinkled and worn from constant wear and tear over a ten-year period, with his back the only visible sign of a human being squeezed in a school desk combo plonked DS, slightly left of center.*

Losser: *(Holds up a tabloid. Headline reads: 'Justice for the Babysitter Killer?')* They don't care who they pin this on.

Lights up full.

So weary of responsibility that he could do this job in his sleep, **Judge Powers**, *a venerable master of the legal system, sits behind a bench six-feet high, CS. Directly below is a chaise-longue, with a day-glo flowery pattern. Here reclines the overly eager to please 20-something Mister* **Stenographer**, *dressed as if on holiday in Bermuda shorts, garish Hawaiian shirt and flip-flops. He furiously types away throughout the trial on a laptop, taking a sip from a pina colada in an outrageously tall* *and flamboyant cocktail glass.*

DSR, an empty desk runs the width of the wall. A comfy leather chair awaits its sitter. The belligerent **State Prosecutor** *enters and exits the stage continually, unless examining a witness, to gather a new set of ammunition and re-enters with arms full of volumes of heavy books for further sifting.*

The witness stand is symbolised by a white gate enclosure that extends out from the left-hand side of the judge's bench, USL. The **DNA Expert**, *45, stands alert within the white picket fence. She is a force to be reckoned with: a hardline feminist, she sees herself as an angel of legal truth, sympathetic to any suspect bullied by the patriarchal privilege of male authority, demonstrated via unlawful interrogation practices.*

Judge Powers: Court's in session. Quiet in the gallery.

Stenographer: *(Reads from laptop)* In this third hearing of The Babysitter Murder Trial, that being the State versus yet another dastardly criminal, biased by our social fears and stigmas, the defendant, Mr Losser, Inmate No. 66660067, dismissed free public counsel upon petition, which was deemed acceptable by presiding Judge Powers, so that he might present witnesses in his own defense. Before a short recess, DNA Expert was being questioned by the State Prosecutor: 'No, it is not our conclusion that Mr Losser's DNA could have been found on the victim's undergarments, although, yes, his fingerprints were found in one corner of the young girl's panties.'

Losser: Is it in your opinion that I could possibly have committed this crime?

by Shorelle Cole

DNA Expert: No, DNA Expert and Co are of the opinion that, upon discovering the victim's dead body, when you ran the sweat from your palms against that of her wrists to check her pulse, your DNA was deposited directly onto the skin. Similar transfer occurred when you held the babysitter to your chest, in an attempt to pacify her with a hug in a moment of trauma, despite the fact her time of death was much earlier.

Judge Powers: *(To the **State Prosecutor**)* You wish to cross-examine?

State Prosecutor: *(Unable to take his eyes off a most fascinating piece of writing in one of the thick volumes he has just opened)* Do you honestly expect us to believe that the convict ...

DNA Expert: 'He' has a name.

State Prosecutor: *(Reflects upon what he just read. Tilts his head upwards as if comprehension will drip from the walls)* Do you honestly expect intelligent people of this fine State represented in the gallery, for the judge and a jury of the defendant's peers ... expect us to believe that DNA found on the personal clothing of the murder victim was the result of a careless act by someone in shock upon discovery of brutalised human remains? An act that he very well carried out himself? Surely yours is a subjective emotional conjecture rather than an objective scientific opinion by an expert in the field of deoxyribonucleic acid?

DNA Expert: You're accusing me of ... why you're insulting my femininity.

State Prosecutor: *(Head back in the books)* I'm done questioning the witness, your Honour.

Blackout.

Lights up.

Judge Powers: *(To **Stenographer**)* When are you on holiday?

Stenographer: *(Campy)* Next week. I feel as if I'm already there. Care to see the brochure of where we'll be staying?

Judge Powers: Love to.

Stenographer *steps back a few paces, expands laptop for the judge to view.*

Stenographer: It's got its own beach. And we've signed up for ...

Losser: I'd like to ask for Starr to take the witness box.

Stenographer: *(Loudly whispers)* I'll show you soon as we finish up here.

Annoyed, he snaps the computer shut and reclines back on the chaise-longue. Once settled, he reopens it and starts to type.

The Babysitter, Starr, *wearing shorts and a sleeveless T-shirt, walks barefooted into the witness box. Her long hair is pulled back into a single ponytail. A young woman, her peculiarly lean physique could be mistaken for anorexia. She looks slightly disheveled as if she's been training for a triathlon or been in a street fight.*

by Shorelle Cole

Starr: *(Plays Cat's Cradle with a found piece of elastic she's made into a finger rope toy)* Why, hello, Mr Losser. Never ever thought I'd see you again. How's that pretty girlfriend of yours?

Losser: We broke up a long time ago, Starr.

Starr: That's too bad. I think romance is grand. Don't you think romance is grand, Mr Losser?

Blackout.

Lights up.

Judge Powers: Please read the witness's testimony.

Stenographer: *(From the chaise-longue)* 'My name is Starr. I am the babysitter for the two kids, Marybelle and Joseph-Paul, who live with their mommy on 222 New Prospect Road.

'A man lets himself into the chain link fence on the property and says he knows me but he's lying 'cos I ain't ever seen him before. He watches me from across the street in his car. I'm kind of scared 'cos I see him sweating from how hot it must be in his car. I see him from the porch where I read my romance novel. He comes out of that car when he sees me get up and run around the yard looking for Marybelle and Joseph-Paul. He just lets the fence bang shut behind him, and I say "please, mister, go away before their mother comes back and gets mad 'cos you shouldn't be on her property".

'He says he knew their mom and that he's gonna help me look for Marybelle and Joseph-Paul. And I catch them giggling, hiding under the porch, waiting for me to find them. Playing a game, see? This strange man, he follows me inside and says he'll help put the two kids to bed when they both fall asleep watching TV.

'It's dark outside now and I'm about to call home, and get my big sister Judy to come over. He holds down the phone thingamyjiggy and knocks me to the ground, and hangs up the phone. I scream like a fire engine. He punches me in my mouth real hard and tells me not to wake up the kids. He gets out his dick and dirties me, so I'm not a good girl anymore. I start balling my eyes out again, and he crunches my jaw somehow, slapping me over and over: "Shut up, bitch." That's not a very nice thing to say to a person …

'He disappears for awhile and I think I'm scot-free when I hear the screen door slam shut. But after a while he comes back upstairs to finish me off, I guess, 'cos he stabs me again and again with a cake knife from the kitchen. He's getting so mad 'cos he's picked a blunt knife. The dummy. I thought I was gonna faint before he looked me in the eye, and says "my arm's tired". He left me alone after that. And that's my story.'

Judge Powers: You wish to cross-examine?

State Prosecutor: *(Setting up three easels)* How old are you, Starr?

by Shorelle Cole

Starr: I'm 21. I'm legal now. Can you imagine? I could go drinking, if things were different.

State Prosecutor: 21. Would you say you have a good memory?

Starr: S'pose so. I dunno.

State Prosecutor: What was the last thing you ate for supper?

Starr: Golly, that's a tough one. It was so long ago.

State Prosecutor: Exactly my point, Starr. You've been dead now for … what? Ten years?

Starr: I was 11 when I was killed, yeah, so, yeah, I'm 21 now. So, yeah, it was ten years ago.

State Prosecutor: And you are sure – 100 percent certain – that this man, Mr Losser, is not the man who killed you?

Starr: I may not remember what I had for dinner, mister, but I can tell you that Mr Losser is one of the nicest men I ever met. And one more thing I can tell you: Mr Losser was not the man who killed me. A person doesn't forget the last moments of their life. Everything is so clear that that situation haunts you 'til there ain't no more Earth or sun or moon. Or the stars.

Blackout.

Lights up.

Losser: *(Stands behind the picket fence. He picks his nose, shifts his groin with his hands down his trousers.)* Like I said in the other two trials, I was a neighbor of the two little kids Starr babysat.

State Prosecutor: If you lived next door, why is it that you didn't see this man Starr spoke of come onto the property? You heard no disturbance whatsoever while the babysitter was being attacked?

Losser: I dunno. It was late when I came home.

State Prosecutor: Later than your set curfew?

Losser: I was home in time for the conditions on my parole.

State Prosecutor: You're on parole for multiple counts of child pornography, isn't that correct, Mr Losser?

Losser: I'm not proud of the man I once was. But I never killed that babysitter. Starr sat here, sworn before God Almighty, and told you so herself.

Blackout.

Lights up.

State Prosecutor: *(Places a blank canvas against each of the easels. A sermon to the audience, his flock of gullible believers)* In summation, I won't bore the jury with words. Instead, I allow this pictorial evidence to justify the State's sentencing this man twice before, to the only vengeful yet merciful recourse, the death penalty.

by Shorelle Cole

State Prosecutor (CONT'D): At the second hearing of this infamous case – the sexual assault and brutal murder of an 11-year-old girl, babysitting at the home of two, also vulnerable, nursery school children – at that second hearing, Mr Losser attempted to blame the State for a coerced self-confession. Now, at his third and final hearing, Mr Losser would have us believe that his obvious presence at the scene of the crime was due to good neighborly conduct, and not in any way symptomatic of his barbaric, pornographic intentions towards the babysitter. I know some of you may feel that the babysitter's version of events should exonerate Mr Losser of any criminal involvement in her death.

Nice one. Nice one. All I ask is that you, the Jury, give equal weighting to Exhibit A *(Taps on first canvas)*: this colour close-up of the abdominal area exposing ripped-open bits of intestine, stomach, and broken pelvic bone. Equal weighting to Exhibit B *(Taps on second canvas)*: a colour close-up of the babysitter's bruised mouth and dislocated jaw. And, equal weighting to Exhibit C: a panoramic view of the bedroom crime scene. The man who did this knew what he was doing. The man who did this deserves no sympathy. The man who did this rests easily in our mind with no unreasonable doubt of his guilt.

Judge Powers: The Jury may be excused to deliberate.

Lights fade out.

THE END

Shorelle Cole is working on the completion of her MA Scriptwriting dissertation, *Vivaldi's Mistresses*, about the classical composer's elite corps of orphan musicians; an all-female orchestra and choir for whom he composed the majority of performance works including *Gloria*, *The Four Seasons* and operatic scores.

by Shorelle Cole

Beth Crane

Photographs
An Animated Short

FADE IN:

EXT. MEADOW – DAY

A meadow, mid-afternoon in high summer. The sun glints in a bright blue sky. Birdsong and distant laughter fill the air.

LUCY, 8, crouches over a daisy. She wears a bright white dress and a straw hat. Around her neck is a battered old Polaroid camera on a cracked leather strap.

With a whirr-click, she takes a photograph. She shakes it, looks at it with a smile and then tosses it over her shoulder.

It lands on the grass behind her. The photograph is beautiful – perfectly framed, balanced and focused. She ignores it, goes to take another.

KEITH, 9, in shorts and a stained shirt, watches her from a distance. He shields his eyes from the sun, sees the photograph on the ground. He watches it as it flutters towards him in a light breeze. Dashing towards it, he catches the picture and stares at it.

Lucy has moved on, leaving a trail of photographs behind her. She moves from plant to plant like a butterfly, pausing only to take a picture before moving on to the next.

Leaving space between them, Keith begins to follow her, to collect the photographs. She doesn't notice.

INT. KEITH'S BEDROOM – DUSK

An attic room, battered furniture. At a desk below an open window, Keith looks through the photographs. He spreads them out over the desk, caresses them with his fingertips. He lifts a photograph of a ladybird to his face, closes his eyes and inhales, deeply.

There is a jamjar of wilted flowers resting on his windowsill, just out of reach. He reaches for it, manages to nudge it down into his hand. He takes a battered daisy, compares it with the photograph and finds it wanting. He crushes the petals with clumsy fingers, tips the jar into the bin, flowers, water and all.

EXT. MEADOW – DAY

Lucy is hunched over a fallen tree, photographing the bugs that are crawling from the inside. She grins, pokes the dead wood with a twig and watches them emerge, taking photograph after photograph.

Keith approaches her from the path. In his hands he holds the photographs, fanned out. He taps her on the shoulder.

She looks up at him, then at the photographs. She smiles, dismisses them. He holds them out again.

She pulls him forwards to look through the viewfinder on her camera. He takes a photograph, with her guidance. She hands it to him, smiling. He looks down at the photograph – clumsy, slightly fuzzy but not terrible – and then at her.

He snatches the camera from her, breaking the strap. He runs and runs.

by Beth Crane

Lucy stares after him, bewildered. She begins to cry.

EXT. MEADOW – DUSK

Keith, reaching the other side of the meadow, slows to a stop. He pants, leaning his hands on his knees to gulp in air.

He looks down at the camera in his hands, smiles and strokes it with a finger. A dandelion catches his eye and he crouches in front of it, takes a photograph. He waits for it to emerge from the camera and then shakes it, impatiently.

The photograph is a blur. He shakes it again but nothing changes.

He takes a photograph of a nearby tree, waits for it to develop. It is wonky, badly framed. He takes another and another, discarding every one in frustration. Each is worse than the last.

Holding the strap he slings the camera onto his shoulder, starts walking.

EXT. BRIDGE – DUSK

Babbling water – a river. Keith, walking over the bridge, is startled by the beauty of the sunset. He looks up at it, marvelling, then raises the camera. He takes a photograph.

The photograph is terrible. It ruins the beauty of the evening. Bursting into angry sobs, he flings first the photograph and then the camera into the river with a splash before running from the scene.

From the banks, Lucy watches him.

When he is gone, she hitches up her dress and wades into the river. She digs in the mud with her hands, fishing for the camera.

She slips, half-falls into the water. Her white dress filthy, she stands up again. Caught in some nearby debris, she sees her camera. She pulls it from the tangle.

She tips it and a stream of water pours out. She presses the button and the camera emits a miserable whirr. She sighs.

Defeated and barefoot, she clambers onto the bank and begins to walk home, dangling the camera by its broken strap.

INT. KITCHEN – NIGHT

Lucy's kitchen. The camera is dissected, spread out in pieces on newspaper. A crackling fire renders the components a glinting, flickering orange.

EXT. FIELD – DAY

Another glorious afternoon. Lucy, wearing a blue cotton dress, holds her camera again. The strap, knotted back together, is wound repeatedly around her wrist.

She crouches over a butterfly, photographs it. The photograph whirrs from the camera. It is just as beautiful as the others she has taken. From the branches of a tree, Keith watches her. She puts the photograph into her pocket and walks away.

FADE OUT.

THE END

....

Beth Crane once won a mug in a writing competition. Spurred on by a love of crockery she took up scriptwriting but has unfortunately won very little since. She now mostly works with puppets.

by Beth Crane

Georgina Kuna

The HeArt of The Matter
An extract from a TV sitcom in development

When faced with stiff competition for an office job, prim, middle-aged Joy inadvertently agrees to be a life model at the small 'HeArt of the Matter' arts centre. Unfortunately, young, attractive Savannah grabs the receptionist's job before Joy can explain the misunderstanding.

Joy discovers the life model pay is great, and that life drawing tutor Gilbert, is devastatingly attractive. But, when Gilbert reveals his real passion is taxidermy, and Joy realises that he has a sack containing something that is clearly still alive, she decides to leave. While she is hidden behind a screen, supposedly undressing to model, the life class, a small group of old ladies, arrives. She overhears them giggling about Bob's modelling 'assets' or rather, his lack of them. She persuades Beryl, the oldest, to model instead, dressed modestly in a toga.

Meanwhile, in the canteen, Gilbert arm-wrestles with Hazel the cook, to win a space in her freezer for his latest taxidermy project. Bob, the centre manager, arrives with Savannah, and Hazel rushes off to get her latest amazing coffee and walnut cake. Savannah tells Bob and Gilbert she can't eat it, as she's watching her weight, and is allergic to nuts. But Hazel has an anger management problem, particularly when it comes to cake refusals.

Gilbert goes to get help before Hazel finds out Savannah won't eat her cake. He finds Delphine, the ceramics and painting tutor who has a penchant for alternative therapy, in reception. She has blocked the exit, and Joy's escape, with a stack of paintings, and roped Joy in to help her hang new ones. Despite the urgency of his mission, Gilbert stops to contemplate Delphine's new work ...

INT – RECEPTION – DAY

Joy supports a large painting with trembling arms. It is just like all the other pictures on the walls. Her face is hidden. Delphine contemplates it seriously.

Gilbert bursts in, clutching a bunch of lavender.

> **GILBERT**
> There you are, there's a bit of a situation in the canteen ... oooh, new work?

> **DELPHINE**
> Yes, I know, a completely new direction for me. What do you think?

They stand and contemplate. Joy can't hold the picture up any longer and lowers it. She simpers guiltily at Gilbert.

> **GILBERT**
> Oh, I see you've met Joy, our new life model.

INT – CANTEEN – DAY

Hazel emerges from behind the serving hatch carrying an extravagant and gigantic cake. She presents it with a flourish.

by Georgina Kuna

> **HAZEL**
> Ta da!

> **SAVANNAH**
> Oh, isn't it lovely? But, I'm sorry, I really can't have any.

Hazel puts the cake down carefully.

> **HAZEL**
> Say that again?

> **SAVANNAH**
> It's the nuts, honestly, I can't.

Bob steps between them.

> **BOB**
> Now now Hazel ... remember ...

Hazel raises a silencing finger. Bob cringes. Hazel wordlessly disappears behind the serving hatch.

> **BOB**
> ... anger management techniques.
> Well done Hazel!

He relaxes.

> **SAVANNAH**
> Why does she need anger ...

Cries of rage and crashing crockery burst from the serving hatch.

INT – RECEPTION – DAY

Joy is looking very sheepish.

DELPHINE
Oh, I see! You'll love working with Gilbert, dear. He's quite the gentleman.

Gilbert grins. He is absurdly flattered. He holds out the lavender to Delphine.

GILBERT
Thank you very much Delphine. Here, this is for you.

She takes the lavender and sniffs it.

DELPHINE
You see? How sweet of you Gilbert.

GILBERT
Oh God! I almost forgot. Hazel is about to offer cake to the new girl.

DELPHINE
Cake? Lovely, what flavour?

GILBERT
Coffee and walnut. My favourite actually.

JOY
Really? Mine too!

DELPHINE
Well, time for a tea break then!

GILBERT
No! The new girl can't eat it. She's allergic to nuts!

DELPHINE
WHAT?

GILBERT
You try and calm her down with the lavender, I'll get a cookery book.

DELPHINE
Good thinking.

She sails out.

GILBERT
You should take something too.

He grabs a hideously 'erotic' jug, with a handle like a large erection, and shoves it into Joy's hands. She doesn't notice the erotic imagery.

GILBERT
Quick! Before it's too late.

Joy looks to the exit. It's still totally blocked. She wanders after him.

JOY
If she's not going to eat the cake then what's the hurry?

INT – CANTEEN – DAY

Bob and Savannah are lashed to the top of a table. Hazel hovers over them, a large slice of cake in one huge fist, a voodoo doll made of ham and other savoury stuff, in the other.

Gilbert and Delphine circle her. Delphine brandishes the lavender and chants; Gilbert hefts a large hardback book. Hazel keeps her eyes on them.

Bob manages to grab a table knife and saws at Savannah's bonds. Hazel takes a huge bite of cake, then bites the head off the voodoo doll.

> **GILBERT**
> Sweet and savoury together. She's really losing it, we can't wait much longer.

> **DELPHINE**
> Try a recipe, quick. Quick!

Gilbert flicks through the book.

> **GILBERT**
> Hazel. Listen, a nice recipe for biscuits ...

Hazel freezes. Her face turns bright red.

> **GILBERT**
> ... sugar, flour, vanilla ... extra virgin olive oil ... Olive oil? Yuck!

by Georgina Kuna

DELPHINE
Who is that book by?

GILBERT
Ermmm, errrr, Heston Blumenthal ...?
Oh dear ...

Bob saws frantically at Savannah's bonds with the knife.

Hazel erupts and dives at Gilbert. He clouts her round the head with the book. The slice of cake flies up, sticks to the ceiling. Hazel falls back, out cold, on top of Bob and Savannah.

BOB
Christ, even Worrall Thompson would've been better.

Joy enters.

JOY
Oh my God! Are they alive?

SAVANNAH
Help, please help. I can't breathe.

Joy walks over to her.

JOY
Well, we could do a deal I suppose ...

SAVANNAH
What?

                    JOY
            Ohhh, a little job swap maybe?

                  SAVANNAH
            No. Are you threatening me with
            that ... thing?

                    JOY
            This?

Joy holds the jug up. She almost drops it when she realises what she's holding. Delphine gasps. Joy gauges her audience.

                    JOY
            ... Art. Obviously, this is incredible
            ... ummm .... mind-boggling ... Art!

Delphine smiles.

                  DELPHINE
            Thank you dear, you have quite an
            eye.

                  SAVANNAH
            It's disgusting. Now help me out
            from under this great lump.

Delphine scowls.

                  DELPHINE
            That wasn't very kind. Perhaps we
            should have let Hazel finish what
            she'd started.

Joy shrugs and turns away. Savannah squeals furiously. Hazel stirs.

by Georgina Kuna

HAZEL
Why is my cake on the ceiling?

Everyone looks up.

BEGIN SLOW MOTION

The cake peels off the ceiling and falls towards Savannah's face. Joy looks from cake to Savannah to cake.

She hurls the jug away and holds out her hands, catches the cake. Delphine dives toward the falling jug. Savannah flops back, relieved.

Delphine grabs at the handle of the jug but misses.

END SLOW MOTION

HAZEL
Nice catch! Right. Where's that girl who doesn't like cake?

Hazel heaves herself half up, but is like an overturned turtle and can't quite make it.

SAVANNAH
OK OK. You can have the job. I don't want it. I DON'T WANT IT!

Savannah wriggles like crazy and manages to free herself.

BOB
Wow. Brilliant ... we need exactly that kind of determination in our staff.

He drops the knife with a clatter.

> **BOB**
> You're going to fit in here perfectly,
> even if you don't eat cake.

He looks at her expectantly. She looks at him with disdain.

She snatches the book from Gilbert and clouts Hazel, who flops back unconscious, pinning Bob firmly again. She drops the book and stalks out.

Delphine crouches over the broken jug. The old ladies shuffle in.

> **OLD LADY 1**
> Oh is that cake? What flavour?

> **EVERYONE ELSE (IN SYNC)**
> Coffee and walnut.

Joy tastes the mess of cake in her hands.

> **JOY**
> Mmmm, it's reeeeaaaallllyyyy
> goooood.

> **DELPHINE**
> How can you think of cake at a time
> like this?

She holds up the handle of the smashed jug. The old ladies fall about laughing raucously.

Delphine gathers up the pieces and rushes out.

by Georgina Kuna

JOY
Oh dear. She's really upset and it's all my fault. I suppose I should go.

BOB
Oh God, not you as well. Don't spose you fancy the admin job?

JOY
Really? Yes, yes I'd love it ... I'm not really a life model. Sorry.

BOB
That's fine. If you could just help me ...

Joy goes to help him. He grunts and wriggles.

GILBERT
Hang on a minute. What about the life class?

Joy stops helping Bob.

JOY
Well, now you mention it ... the admin pay is a bit low ... you know, compared to the life modelling.

BOB
Shut up Gilbert. Look ... I'll give you £12.00 an hour.

JOY
OK. Deal. Sorry Gilbert.

GILBERT
Ah well. Sorry ladies, looks like Bob's back on modelling duty.

The old ladies groan.

OLD LADY 1
Beryl will be so disappointed.

Bob looks thoroughly offended.

BOB
What? What's wrong with my modelling.

JOY
Oh. Where is Beryl?

OLD LADY 1
She fell asleep, we thought it best to leave her.

Joy takes Gilbert's arm.

JOY
Come with me.

BOB
Come back!

The old ladies gather around the cake, completely ignoring Bob and Hazel.

by Georgina Kuna

BOB
What's wrong with my modelling?

INT – LIFE DRAWING STUDIO – DAY

Beryl is draped across the chaise-longue in her toga. Joy and Gilbert gaze fondly at her.

GILBERT
Oh, I suppose that'll work. She looks very peaceful doesn't she? Nice and still too.

JOY
She does look very peaceful ... very peaceful ... and very, very, very still.

Joy frowns and leans closer.

JOY
Beryl ... Beryl? BERYL? Oh my God, I think she's ... she's dead!

Joy clings to Gilbert in horror. Gilbert looks offended.

GILBERT
Well, I think I know a dead thing when I see it.

JOY
Do something then!

Gilbert leans down and shouts in Beryl's ear.

GILBERT
Beryl! Fancy a bit of coffee and walnut cake?

Beryl stirs, puts a hearing aid in.

BERYL
Did you say cake? Thank you dear, but I prefer a nice plain digestive these days.

INT – RECEPTION – DAY

Joy enters reception. Delphine is hanging something on the wall behind the desk.

JOY
Delphine. That wasn't a great start, I'm really sorry for breaking your jug.

DELPHINE
Oh no need dear, no need. A disaster is nothing less than a new creative opportunity. I should be thanking you for opening my mind to the possibilities. Besides, we needed a clock in here.

Delphine steps back to reveal a mosaic clock made of the pieces of broken jug, using the unbroken (penis-like) handle as the 'big hand'.

DELPHINE
... ask and the universe will provide
... isn't it wonderful?

by Georgina Kuna

                           JOY
                     It's ... really ... er

                        DELPHINE
                     You don't like it?

Delphine looks upset.

                           JOY
                    No no. I do ... I'm just ... well ...
                    speechless.

Delphine smiles indulgently.

                        DELPHINE
                    Aahh. You know, people often are
                    when they see my work, it's really
                    very affirming.

She folds Joy into a warm and rather suffocating embrace. Joy eyes the clock, casts her gaze around at all the other artwork, clearly all by Delphine.

                           JOY
                     It's perfect.

INT – CANTEEN – DAY

Beryl sits sipping tea and nibbling a biscuit.

The old ladies are ranged in a semi-circle around Bob, still pinned, and Hazel, still unconscious, happily sketching. Gilbert peruses their work quietly.

BOB
This is NOT funny.

Hazel stirs. The old ladies freeze, pencils in mid-air. Gilbert grabs the cookery book and raises it. Hazel snorts and shuffles. Bob wriggles free and storms off.

Hazel settles comfortably and snores. Gilbert lowers the book. The old ladies all tut, sigh, and attack their sketches with erasers.

THE END

....

Georgina Kuna lives, works, and writes in Norwich. Scriptwriting achievements include Best Short Script at The End of the Pier International Film Festival 2010, and studying at UEA. She is currently working on a TV sitcom, and an animated family feature.

by Georgina Kuna

Tilly Lunken

Occupy Eric
A Short Play

Adams – (17) is convinced his brains entitle him to lord over everyone. He doesn't need teaching, hell he's a teacher.

Grahams – (17) but less sure of his place in the world, he is ready to follow the lead of whoever is taking the class.

Morrison – (17) and doesn't need teachers as he knows everything there ever needs to be known. Who needs to go to school when you will one day own it?

Eric – (37) is a teacher of much experience, much ingenuity and much patience.

A one-man blue tent is pitched on the edge of a small-town Occupy camp. The zip has been padlocked shut from the outside. In front a pair of dirty Birkenstocks and a pile of clothes; to the side an upturned milk crate topped with a newspaper and a steaming mug of tea. Other crates are scattered and there is a sign proclaiming 'Occupy School.'

The tent moves; someone is trapped inside it.

Adams *and* ***Grahams****, both in school uniform, enter.* ***Grahams*** *kicks the school sign over. The tent stops moving.*

Adams: No teacher. No students. No school.

Grahams: What's it Morrison says? There is education awaiting all who we encounter.

Adams: Ah, but this isn't just about education Grahams. This is about the man in the tent; the everyman who gets too big for his sandals and outgrows societal norms.

Grahams: What, that tent?

He points to the tent.

Adams: No, not that tent! Show me any space left in the world I'll show you a filthy-grubby-left-wing-good-for-nothing-scumbag-junky-squatter 'occupying' it. Now, how about you do something useful? Bring some order to this classroom?

Grahams: Yes, boss.

Adams: I feel Sir will suffice in the current context.

***Grahams** organises the milk crates. **Adams** continues his lecture.*

I am not sure you fully comprehend the extent of the assault on our way of life by this man in a tent.

Grahams: What man in a tent?

Adams: Sir.

Grahams: Sir. I mean there's no one else here, he left his—

by Tilly Lunken

Adams: Take a seat, Grahams. This is a symptom of what is so wrong with contemporary society.

Grahams slumps on a crate.

Grahams: Isn't that the point of all the tents? Sir.

Adams: It is not the point of all the tents. Grahams. Tell me, what would you say to this man?

Grahams: Er ... Hello?

Adams: *(Snort)* Exactly. Now let us turn to this little set-up. What do you see?

Adams gestures towards the newspaper and the tea.

It is *The Guardian*. And if you look at the crossword it will be two thirds completed in black biro. No commitment to finishing.

Grahams: What? The crossword?

Adams: The man who owns this paper might not have a tent that is directly blocking access to a cathedral but he remains a threat to the history of Empire as sure as if he erected his syphilitic canvas on the steps of St Paul's itself. And we can tell this Grahams, by these two objects. We know this man from what he leaves behind.

Grahams: Because he doesn't finish the crossword.

Adams: Yes. And because he leaves his tea.

Adams snatches up the mug and the paper to use as props in his performance.

Grahams: What about the tent? Sir.

*The tent moves, **Adams** doesn't notice but **Grahams** realises that someone must be inside it. **Adams** becomes more caught up in his own importance, preaching.*

Adams: It is the objects that this flea leaves us that conjure up the putrefying dreadlocks that must surely frame a grimy, dirty bespectacled face.

Grahams: But—

Adams: No buts. Look at this abandoned tea as a metaphor for the man who would leave behind society for an anarchistic life reading socialist tracts and eating lentils.

Scrabbling starts from inside the tent.

It is not the politically correct taste in editorial opinion that separates this cad from his betters. It is his tea.

*With one hand **Adams** now raises the mug of tea above his head, conducting the air with the newspaper in the other hand. **Grahams** inspects the tent.*

***Morrison** enters. The others don't notice.*

Morrison: Typical.

by Tilly Lunken

Adams: Grahams, tell me once and for all, if you saw two good students such as ourselves approaching your abode and you had only just finished pouring the finest tradition in the land, would you up and leave; would you scramble to escape the oncoming onslaught of respectability; would you? No. Would you not stay, calmly sipping on your exquisite brew and more importantly *(Pause)* would you not offer tea to your visitors?

***Grahams** removes a penknife from his pocket and slices a small opening down the right side of the tent canvas. A hand pops out through the opening. **Grahams** jumps back. **Morrison** folds his arms.*

Grahams: Er.

Adams: This newspaper was confirmation of my instantaneous character assessment. He that leaves his tea always has something to hide.

***Grahams** makes a slit on the other side of the tent. Another hand appears.*

Grahams! We must tear down the tents that obstruct the continuing progression of our nation.

*With a flourish **Adams** drains the mug of tea. **Morrison** advances on him and snatches the newspaper.*

Morrison: You are not a good student; you never read any newspapers and you're late.

***Adams** splutters out his last mouthful of tea over **Morrison**.*

And, you just drank my tea.

Grahams *surrenders his knife to the tent's gesturing hand.* ***Adams*** *looks down.*

Adams! Have you listened at all? You of all people should know how this works. Look at me! You just drank my tea from my fucking mug, you fucking mug.

Adams: Sorry, Morrison.

Morrison: You will be; fancy waltzing in like you own the place, taking the class and fucking let fly.

A loud ripping comes from the tent, feet appear from the base and it walks forward to find the Birkenstocks. A slash at the top of the tent and ***Eric****'s head appears.*

Morrison: Great.

Eric *has respectable hair and is now effectively wearing the tent. His arms stick straight out at right angles; only as far as his elbows and the base reaches his calves. He returns* ***Grahams****'s knife.*

Adams/
Grahams: Sir?

Eric: I don't suppose you've had a gander at number 26 down Adams, of my two thirds unfinished crossword?

Eric *awkwardly bends to reach into the tent to find his glasses.*

Grahams: Sir!

by Tilly Lunken

Adams: This is not happening.

Morrison: Oh it is. And he's gone and mucked about my big entrance. I was just getting started. Who does he think he is to come popping out of a tent like that?

Grahams: Morrison? What the hell is going on here?

Eric: Does someone mind helping me put on my glasses?

Grahams takes Eric's glasses and affixes them on Eric's nose.

Adams: Exactly. Is there any reason why old Mr Stevens here just happens to have been conveniently zipped up and out of sight?

Grahams: Oh man, this is such a set-up.

Morrison: No it isn't.

Grahams: I just sliced a teacher out of a tent!

Morrison: You shouldn't have. I dealt with the problem and then he just had to go and decide to get involved.

Adams: Yeah, but he made you tea!

Morrison: How did you—

Adams: Morrison, if that tea really was yours then I bet my own ass that you didn't make it.

Morrison: Fuck off.

Eric coughs.

Eric: I don't feel that sort of language is appropriate for my classroom.

Morrison: This is not your classroom, mate. Here you're just a fucking hippy wearing a tent.

Eric: I'm a fucking teacher wearing a tent. Sit down!

The boys automatically respond to his command.

Eric: So here we are again, back in school without an original thought between the lot of you.

*Morrison, **Grahams** and **Adams** burst into schoolboy joviality.*

Adams: School, Sir?

Morrison: But where are the students, Sir?

Adams: Yes the students, Sir.

Grahams: We're not real students, Sir!

Adams: A school has got to have students, Sir.

Morrison: Or it isn't a school at all, Sir!

Grahams: Is it, Sir?

Eric: I'd prefer it if you called me Eric.

Morrison: You wouldn't be a proper teacher then, Sir.

by Tilly Lunken

Pause.

Eric: Am I a proper teacher?

Grahams: You certainly taught me all about numeracy, Sir!

Eric: Maths? Grahams, you never took in one formula.

Adams: He's precocious like that.

Morrison: Aren't we all?

Eric: Yes. All of you are politically extravagant, insolent boys. I should be forcing Occupy leaflets into your fists and watching you march off into the sunset to educate the world.

Morrison: Oh, take your leaflets and jam them tight.

Eric: So I can shit them out again?

Adams: Seriously though, Sir. Why are you here?

Eric: To escape you lot.

Morrison: Come off it. Teachers don't normally get off this way.

Eric: You want a proper answer?

Morrison: No.

Adams: Yes, Sir.

Grahams: Please, Sir.

Eric: I had thought I'd left my material life behind when I left the school. All I am is this tent. All I needed is the paper and my tea. Ha! But listening to you systematically build a picture of me and now to watch myself relapse so easily back into familiar patterns ... I am not sure at all.

Adams gets to his feet mimicking Eric in his tent, doing silly poses with the milk crates.

Adams: To be honest, it says more about you that you are trying to be serious and make a point, all teacher-like, whilst wearing a tent. Look, your arms stick out all weird!

Grahams and Morrison join in Adams's fun.

Morrison: Yes! You almost had us then, Sir.

Adams: Being so serious, Sir.

Grahams: Careful, Sir!

Morrison: We'll believe anything, Sir!

Adams: You do look a bit Christ-like in that get-up Sir.

Morrison: Tent Jesus, Sir.

Grahams: It's the arms, Sir!

Eric: That is enough. Sit down. Now! Listen for once.

Grahams, Adams and Morrison drop their silly poses and sit back on the crates.

by Tilly Lunken

Eric rolls up his tent sleeves.

Eric: Adams, you slithered in here knowing exactly where you were from, exactly who you were and exactly what you were going to be. Now you are not so sure. Are you? You spend your life judging people by their politics and your idea of normal. You want to teach them how to be normal. How does all this fit into that cup of tea?

Adams looks down at the empty mug still in his hands.

Eric: Morrison, you also know where you stand. You like to stand, don't you, Morrison, when others are sitting in front of you? But not to teach, never to teach, for it's even better to have them lying flat with their faces knocked sideways. You like to be prepared. Which is why when I met you earlier, you stole my clothes before you locked me up in my tent. Nice. Your grandkids are going to love you, Morrison.

Morrison puts his hands in his pockets.

Eric: Then lastly there is you Grahams. Isn't there? Always last. Always, always last. It's all you know, and it's all you'll ever know unless you throw the ball back once in a while. That's why you watch though, isn't it? Notice it all.

Grahams: Yes Sir.

*The boys sullenly regard **Eric** as he tries to sit down on a crate. He falls off it and onto the ground, his arms and legs flailing. **Grahams** helps him to sit up.*

Eric: I know you all far too well. More than myself if I'm honest. Bloody hell. What am I doing here? Honest to God. I need a drink.

Pause. The boys exchange looks.

Adams: Morrison could make us tea.

Morrison: Fat chance.

Pause.

Grahams: So what now?

Adams: We could finish off the crossword?

Eric: Excellent suggestion boys. It may turn into a surprising pleasure to have uniformed students in this classroom after all. Pause. Hang on, why aren't you all in school?

Adams: I think we are, Eric.

THE END

....

Tilly Lunken writes for the theatre. Originally from Melbourne, she also consults as a dramaturg and a script assessor, devises work and loves theatre theory and criticism. If not backstage, you'll find her in the audience – probably in the stalls as her eyes aren't that good.

by Tilly Lunken

Waleed Marzouk

The Blue Corner
A Short Film

OVER BLACK:

We hear knuckles rapping on window glass.

FADE IN:

INT. BOOTH/ PARKING LOT/ TD SPORTS ARENA – NIGHT

NATE (43) – tough years etched on a handsome face – in a tracksuit and blood-stained hoodie, is passed out under the desk. He twitches, his eyes flicker.

NATE'S DREAM:

EXT. WOODS – NIGHT

Nate chases a woman. He breathes heavily, branches scratch his face. She loses her footing, recovers, keeps running. She looks back – it's too dark to see her face. She screams. Nate tackles her.

DREAM ENDS

INT. BOOTH – NIGHT

The rapping on the glass grows insistent.

                    BILLY (OS)
            (hissing)
            Hey! Wake up!

Nate wakes with a start. He sees BILLY (27), the gaunt, bug-eyed ticket booth attendant, through the window. Nate gets to his knees, crouching low, unlocks the door.

                    BILLY
            What the fuck, you fall asleep?

Billy sits on the steps outside, removes the plastic bags wrapped around his shoes. Nate peers out of the window.

                    NATE'S POV

Outside the arena's back entrance, POLICEMEN sip coffee in the snow, idling around three black-and-whites and an ambulance. Whatever's going on, the urgency has died down.

                    BILLY (OS)
            It's all taken care of.

Billy removes his rubber gloves, steps inside the booth. He fishes keys out of his pocket. Nate takes the keys, still staring out.

                    BILLY
            Now what?

Nate unzips his gym bag and changes his hoodie. Billy switches on a small radio – it's tuned to the fight broadcast.

by Waleed Marzouk

> **NORM (RADIO)**
> Well, it's official, Nate Florian is nowhere to be found. Complete radio silence out there. Thirty minutes to fight time! What do you think, Lon? Is this some kind of stunt?

> **LON (RADIO)**
> I don't know, Norm. What I do know is no one wants to miss this. It's been almost two years since he last stepped into the cage after his loss to Raphael Dos Santos. The bookies have tonight's fight at a crippling 7-to-1. Does he have the mental game, at his age—

Nate switches off the radio.

> **NATE**
> I'm going back in.

> **BILLY**
> What now?

> **NATE**
> Call Leo.

Billy looks distressed.

> **BILLY**
> Where's my money?

INT. CORRIDOR/ TD SPORTS ARENA – NIGHT

Nate walks down a stark white corridor flanked by jowly PAULIE (38), grizzled PETE (67), LEO's henchmen, who wear security jackets. Their footsteps echo. Beyond the walls, the ARENA CROWD cheers.

> **PAULIE**
> Tried to make a run for it, huh?
> Fuckin' low life. It's Leo's own fault.
> Handing money over to some over-
> the-hill Southie loser.

Nate faces Paulie. Paulie reaches for his pistol but Nate closes the distance between them before Paulie can draw. Paulie quivers, does his best to mask it.

> **PAULIE (CONT'D)**
> Yeah, tough guy. Give me a reason.

Nate stares Paulie down. Pete watches, bemused.

> **PAULIE (CONT'D)**
> This is gonna be so good. What do you think Leo's gonna do? Better yet, who do you think he's gonna have do it to you?

Nate walks on.

> **PAULIE (CONT'D)**
> Yellow-bellied piece of shit.

INT. LEO'S OFFICE/ TD SPORTS – NIGHT

Nate enters with Paulie and Pete.

by Waleed Marzouk

LEO (43), dapper, sits behind an over-sized desk, tissue paper tucked under his collar. An ASSISTANT powders his bald head. DETECTIVE CONSTANCE REARDEN (52) sits across from Leo. Her cold eyes have seen it all. Leo offers Nate a seat. Nate doesn't take it. The fight broadcast plays on a large plasma TV.

RING ANNOUNCER (ON TV)
Ladies and gentlemen: WE. ARE. LIVE! From the sold out TD Garden Arena in Boston, Massachusetts.

Leo clicks his fingers – Paulie turns the sound down.

LEO (TO NATE)
You've got balls. I'll give you that.

Leo looks for a reaction from Nate, gets none.

LEO (CONT'D)
Nate, this is Connie. She's with the BPD's homicide unit. She's here to make sure everything's copacetic.

REARDEN
Hi Nate. My boy Billy's a big fan.

Nate stares down Rearden – she doesn't flinch from his gaze.

LEO
So that house you put a down payment on. With my money. You know I own the property. The most intelligent fighter in the history of the sport. And still a meathead.

Leo chuckles. Nate remains impassive.

> **LEO (CONT'D)**
> Got messy with that girl, huh?

> **NATE**
> It's why I'm here. You can have her back.

Leo laughs.

> **LEO**
> You would do that for me?

A tense beat.

> **LEO (CONT'D)**
> What'd she say? Tell me what she said when you laid out your rosy future together.

Nate struggles to say something, can't find the words.

FLASHBACK BEGINS: EARLIER THAT NIGHT:

EXT. PARKING LOT/ TD SPORTS ARENA – NIGHT

Snow swirls furiously in the howling wind. Nate smokes next to his run-down Mustang convertible, gazing into the woods beyond.

KLARA (26) – coquettish eyes, red ring-girl outfit – approaches from the arena's back entrance. She ends a call and stops at a safe distance.

by Waleed Marzouk

KLARA
You have exactly two minutes.

NATE
What're you doing? Come here.

KLARA
This is close enough.

NATE
So I'm not shouting like some crazy person.

KLARA
You know I filed that restraining order, right?

NATE
Yeah, I know.

KLARA
I'm not fucking around, Nate. I filed it last week.

Nate walks towards her.

NATE
I know. I'm not mad.

KLARA
Right there's fine.

Nate doesn't stop, slowly circles around her.

NATE
All that stuff. Randy, everything.
That's all behind us now.

KLARA
What do you want?

NATE
I got something for you.

An awkward beat.

KLARA
Am I supposed to guess?

NATE
It's in the car.

Klara turns, starts walking back. Nate cuts her off.

NATE (CONT'D)
Wait!

Klara stops. Nate stands between her and the entrance. He digs keys out of his pocket, holds them up.

KLARA
What's that?

NATE
Our house. In the Cape. Right on the water like you said.

KLARA
Have you lost it completely?

A tense beat.

> **NATE**
> You know she got the kids, right?
> I can't see them anymore. No
> weekends, no nothing.

> **KLARA**
> Fuck your kids. I don't care anymore.
> You understand?

Nate's eyes turn cold – it's a familiar sight.

Klara steps back, fumbles with her speed dial, drops the phone.

> **NATE**
> Don't run. The cameras.

Klara makes a run for it, screams. There's no one around to hear. Nate chases after her. She screams louder. Nate gains on her. She dashes into the woods.

FLASHBACK ENDS

INT. OFFICE – NIGHT

Nate sees Leo's smug grin, remembers where he is.

> **NATE**
> She can be ... unreasonable.

> **LEO**
> Not anymore.

NATE
What do you mean?

Rearden laughs.

LEO
Nate. Who do think you're talking to here?

The assistant adds the finishing touches, checks her watch.

ASSISTANT
Ten minutes to ESPN, Mr Fanelli.

LEO (TO NATE)
This wasn't just a hot piece of ass to sully with my fuckstick.

(TO REARDEN)
Sorry, Connie. Locker talk.

(TO NATE)
I invested in that one. A publicist, agent. *Sports Illustrated, Playboy*. Who do you think got her that ad with Revlon? You killed a real fucking cash cow.

Nate looks at Rearden – she smirks.

LEO (CONT'D)
Anyway, I digress. What was I saying?

PAULIE
Revlon, boss.

by Waleed Marzouk

LEO
Shut the fuck up, Paulie.

Leo stands up, walks to a floor mirror, checks himself.

LEO (CONT'D) (TO NATE)
Look. The truth is we need you. We overshot with this one. Bet the whole house. Connie and I were just saying. We need a guy who can last a round with the heathen. It's better if you go down in the second. Shut the gaming commission up if they get lippy.

Nate doesn't respond.

LEO (CONT'D)
I want to hear the words.

NATE
I came back, didn't I?

LEO
You can't fuck around this time, Nate. You have to go down. There'll be a lot more than a dead girl to answer for.

Nate heads to the door.

LEO (CONT'D)
Hold on.

> PAULIE
>
> You want me to keep an eye on him, boss?
>
> LEO
>
> Like you kept an eye on him tonight?
>
> PAULIE
>
> But boss …
>
> LEO (TO NATE)
>
> I wanted you to see this.

Leo nods to Pete. Pete draws a pistol with a silencer and shoots Paulie. Paulie drops to the ground, a clean entry wound in his forehead trickles blood.

Nate looks at Rearden.

> REARDEN
>
> Leave a signed cap and T-shirt for my Billy in your locker room. He's a big fan.
>
> LEO
>
> Go forth, Nate. Make us proud.

Nate stands in place, frozen.

INT. WALKWAY/ PREP POINT/ CAGE/ TD SPORTS ARENA – NIGHT

Nate trots down the walkway with his TRAINING TEAM. DELIRIOUS FANS hang over the rail, straining to high-five him, his mind is elsewhere. His walkout song – Creedence Clearwater Revival's *Bad Moon Rising* – blares through the arena. The crowd roars in appreciation.

The PRESENTERS are pumped up – these are the moments they live for:

> **LON (OS)**
> Two-time NCAA Division-I All-American, the hall-of-famer, the people's champ – 'Noble' Nate Florian!

The crowd chants: FLO-RI-AN!! FLO-RI-AN!!

> **LON (OS)**
> They love him, Norm.

> **NORM (OS)**
> He is a true ambassador of the sport, Lon. One of the classiest guys you'll ever meet and an outstanding well-rounded fighter.

Nate arrives at the prep point. He strips down to his shorts, flexes as a CUTMAN inspects him.

Leo and Pete sit in the front row behind the point.

> **NORM (CONT'D)(OS)**
> An elite wrestler, he likes to press guys up against the cage and break their will. But he hasn't fought in over eighteen months and in Jensen he faces a vicious striker with brutal knockout power.

Nate stomps up the steps to the cage. He slaps his arms, his chest, shadow boxes.

> **NORM (CONT'D)(OS)**
> Make no mistake about it, Lon. Nate will be looking to close the distance, get this fight to the ground and submit Jensen.

Nates looks across the cage at his opponent, STEVEN 'THE HEATHEN' JENSEN (35), a beast covered in jail tattoos. Nate eyeballs him.

The RING ANNOUNCER steps into the centre of the cage.

> **RING ANNOUNCER (INTO MIC)**
> And now, the moment MMA fans across the world have all been waiting for. This is the main event of the evening.

The crowd erupts again – they chant Nate's name.

> **RING ANNOUNCER (CONT'D)**
> Fighting out of the blue corner, the challenger. Weighing in at two hundred and five pounds. Holding a professional record of nineteen wins, seven losses. The former light heavyweight champion. Boston's own—

Jensen hops from one foot to another, winks at Nate.

Blood pounds in Nate's ears, drowns out the arena clamour.

by Waleed Marzouk

FLASHBACK BEGINS:
EXT. WOODS – NIGHT

Nate pins Klara's back to the ground. She screams, scratches at his face, his eyes. He holds down her arms. She screams again. Nate recognises he's crossed a line, no return. His eyes glaze over. He headbutts her, crushes her face. The sound reverberates in his skull. She coughs up blood, broken teeth.

>   **KLARA**
>   **(GURGLING)**
>   Fucking loser.

Nate, heaving, retches.

FLASHBACK ENDS

INT. CAGE – NIGHT

The REFEREE starts the fight.

The fight bell clangs.

>   **REFEREE**
>   Now bring it on!

Nate charges forward, takes control of the centre. They circle, feeling each other out with feints. Jensen throws a spry leg kick. It lands on Nate's thigh with a slap. Nate hops, recovers. Jensen throws the kick again – it finds its home.

Jensen grows confident, cocky. He taunts Nate with raised arms. Jensen feints a jab, throws the kick again. Nate grabs Jensen's foot and counters with a vicious right hook. It lands square on Jensen's jaw – he's out cold.

LON (OS)
Wow! Wow!! JUST. LIKE. THAT!!

Nate jumps on the fence, hollers at the crowd. Their roar is thunderous. The roof is coming off.

Leo seethes. Jubilant fans congratulate him, slap his back. He speaks in Pete's ear. Pete gets up, walks off.

Nate pumps his fists in the air, victorious.

BLEACH OUT TO WHITE

THE END

....

Waleed Marzouk is from Cairo, Egypt, where he has worked as an actor, scriptwriter and journalist.

by Waleed Marzouk

Oliver Michell

The Wheel
For The Stage

Gungulphus – Father of Exodus and Deuteronomy; Inventor of the Wheel; Delusional Philanderer (Elderly).

Mother – Mother of Exodus and Deuteronomy; Wife of Gungulphus; Crudely Virtuous Martyr.

Grandma – Mother of Gungulphus; Nasty Old Woman.

The Mistress – Mistress of Gungulphus; Bitch.

Exodus & **Deuteronomy** – Twin Sons of Gungulphus; Fat Scoundrels.

The action takes place in the Workshop of **Gungulphus**. *Here he perfects his new invention: the wheel. Workbenches are littered with tools. A saw is fixed to the wall by a bracket. Supervision of the workshop takes place from a raised dais, on which stands a clerk's writing desk and high stool.*

A multi-coloured pyramid of Turkish Delight, thickly sprinkled with icing sugar, sits on a workbench.

Attached to a wall is a black crank handle, approximately three feet long.

Night. **Grandma** *sits on the high stool, asleep, her head resting on the desk. Darkness, except for spotlight on the saw and the pyramid of Turkish Delight.*

Centre stage, **Mother**, **Exodus** *and* **Deuteronomy**. *Their heads are trapped between the spokes of a horizontal wheel, approximately six feet in diameter.* **Exodus** *and* **Deuteronomy** *face in one direction,* **Mother**, *the opposite. If* **Mother** *pushes, she will push against* **Exodus** *and* **Deuteronomy**.

Exodus *and* **Deuteronomy** *are asleep, standing.* **Mother** *is attempting to reach the saw. She is at the end of her strength. She stretches towards it, hoping to pull her sons so gently towards it that they will not wake.* **Mother** *freezes, arm outstretched, till she is certain* **Grandma** *is asleep, then continues to inch towards the saw. The plan is working;* **Exodus** *and* **Deuteronomy** *shuffle unknowingly sideways in their sleep.*

Mother's *outstretched hand is a foot away from the saw when the stage is filled with the deafening sound of* **Deuteronomy** *shaking a hand bell. Lights up.*

Deuteronomy: Lies! Deceit! Villainy! Mama is sharp and creeps towards sin!

Exodus: Inching for the saw, she was, Grandma, seeking to split Father's invention.

**Exodus
& Deuteronomy**: *(Dragging their mother back to the centre of the stage)* Back back back-back-back-back-back!

Grandma: *(Leaping with alarming agility from the stool into the centre of the stage, snatching up the tray of Turkish Delight)* Disaster it was, misery and mistake, when my son, The Far-Seeing Gungulphus, took up with the likes of you.

Mother: *(Barely able to speak from exhaustion)* I wanted to ... be free ... to free ... my sons.

by Oliver Michell

Grandma: Listen to Young Deuteronomy! Obey Noble Exodus!

*Grandma crams Turkish Delight into her grandsons' mouths, spreading icing sugar over their faces. They chew and swallow eagerly. She then puts a handful into her own mouth before taunting **Mother** with a piece, which **Grandma** holds just out of reach, before stuffing it into her own mouth.*

They are good boys who love their father's law. There's no need, termagant, to teach them the reckoning of treachery.

Grandma hastens for the crank handle.

Exodus & Deuteronomy: The crank! The crank!

Mother: No ... no ... please ...

*Although there is no visible connection between the crank handle on the wall and the Wheel, the turning of the handle by **Grandma** causes the Wheel to spin, in the direction favouring **Exodus** and **Deuteronomy**. Well fed and facing in the right direction, they dance round, shrieking with pleasure. The **Mother** stumbles backwards, barely able to stay upright.*

*The door to the outside world opens. The **Mistress** and **Gungulphus** enter. The **Mistress** resembles an animated mannequin. **Gungulphus** looks at least as old as **Grandma**, with a long, straggling beard and staring eyes. He wears all-in-one long johns and nightshirt; he appears to have had an attack of diarrhoea some months earlier.*

*Unnoticed by the rest of the cast, The **Mistress** stands with arms folded watching the spinning of the Wheel. **Gungulphus** stumbles to the front of the stage and stares glassy-eyed out into the audience, shaking.*

On seeing the arrival of her son, **Grandma** *stops turning the crank, takes up the tray of Turkish Delight and hastens towards* **The Mistress**. *The Wheel stops spinning.* **Exodus** *and* **Deuteronomy** *come to a stop opposite* **The Mistress**.

Gungulphus: *(Screaming)* Tick tock tick tock.

Deuteronomy: *(Interpreting for the benefit of* **The Mistress***, who does not look at him)* Father welcomes you to our house.

Exodus: Home, Deuteronomy. Father said he welcomes you to our home.

Gungulphus: On the one hand, on the other.

Deuteronomy: Father says, you are our mother now.

A howling sob emerges from **Mother**.

Exodus: *(To* **The Mistress***)* Until this night, we have had no mother.

Deuteronomy: Only the guilt of a still breathing womb.

Mother: Who are you? Why are you with my husband?

Exodus: The new mother cannot be expected to interpret this formless grunting.

Grandma: Speak clearly, you are insulting our queen.

The Mistress: I am the Mistress.

Mother: Whose mistress?

by Oliver Michell

The Mistress: *(Turning towards the **Mother**)* Yours.

Mother: Do you betray me, Gungulphus? You bring a new love before our sons.

Gungulphus: Abracadabra.

Deuteronomy: *(To The Mistress)* Father wishes to show you his invention.

Exodus: Father is a famous inventor.

Deuteronomy: A sea of honest folk have benefited from his guile.

Gungulphus: *(Making a buzzing sound with his lips, increasingly agitated, still staring wildly into the second row of the audience)* Bzzzzzzzzzzzzzzzzzzzzz.

Deuteronomy: Father points out that his invention enjoys myriad applicability.

Gungulphus: Ba, ba, ba-ba-baaaah.

Exodus: Vehicles will be transformed, machines shall spin silkily.

Grandma: Permit me, beloved daughter, to offer you a cube of bright coloured starch. *(She presents the pyramid of Turkish Delight to The Mistress)*. Its flavour is most delicate.

The Mistress takes a piece of Turkish Delight. Holds it between thumb and index finger up in front of her face, inspecting it contemptuously. Having inspected it, she throws it to the floor with disgust. **Grandma,**

Deuteronomy and *Exodus* are filled with awe at this action. *The Mistress*, looking straight ahead, holds out the fingers that touched the Turkish Delight. *Grandma* instantly wipes them gently with a cloth.

The Mistress: By what name shall the marvel be known?

Gungulphus: *(More and more agitated)* Herriga lerriga lerriga.

Deuteronomy: The name shall be famous, a jewel on the lips of men.

Exodus: Its faculties reverenced, its glory unmatched.

Gungulphus: Lerriga herriga-herriga.

Deuteronomy: Father fashioned the name himself, coaxing it to perfection.

Gungulphus: On the one hand on the other.

Exodus: He calls it ...

Deuteronomy: He calls it ...

Deuteronomy & Exodus: THE WHEEL, THE WHEEL

Grandma: *(Spinning round and round, arms in the air)* Wheeeee! Wheeeee!

Mother: *(Bitter, exhausted laughter. Everyone turns to stare at her)* Gungulphus is far-seeing and wise ... but he did not ... invent ... the wheel.

by Oliver Michell

Gungulphus: *(Infuriated, rushing at his wife)* Herriga lerriga lerriga.

Deuteronomy: Father enquires as to why there is no silence from a discarded slattern.

Gungulphus: Lerriga herriga herriga.

Exodus: Father observes that, after harvest time, the ploughed furrow is burnt and turned, folded down to make fertile bed for the fresh seed.

*Exodus smiles ingratiatingly at **The Mistress**, who ignores him.*

The Mistress: I have been taxed enough by this show of family love. I am the Mistress here. And I would see the creature walk.

Gungulphus: On the one hand on the other.

Deuteronomy: Yes, Father, the machine is in perfect order.

Exodus: We are ready, Father, to win our new mother's love.

Gungulphus: *(With excitement, stares out into the audience, spreads his arms wide and shrieks)* Clap clap.

***Deuteronomy** and **Exodus** push as hard as they can on the spokes around their necks but **Mother**, with the last ounce of strength within her, pushes back in the opposite direction. The boys strain against their mother, but cannot shift the Wheel.*

Mother: *(Grunting from the effort)* Your father ... did not ... invent ... the wheel.

The Mistress: Why does it refuse to dance? Give me the starch!

*Grandma rushes to hand her the pyramid of Turkish Delight, which **The Mistress** crams violently into the mouths of **Deuteronomy** and **Exodus**.*

Gungulphus: Starch! Starch!

Grandma seizes a handful of Turkish Delight and crams it into Gungulphus's mouth, dusting his beard with icing sugar.

Grandma: My son Gungulphus opines that, like all machinery, this invented marvel may not be operated by a *(squawked into **Mother**'s face)* foul-faced malignant.

The Mistress: My pleasure is for dancing. Detach the head of the withered womb. Unstopper her; once dead-headed, Gungulphus himself may step into the bowels of the machine.

Gungulphus visibly panics at the suggestion that his own head should go between the spokes of the Wheel; he makes a buzzing sound with his lips.

Deuteronomy: Father observes that he is the overseer.

Exodus: High-minded Deuteronomy mishears. Father calls himself the directing mind.

Deuteronomy: The noble Exodus mishears. Father states that it is impossible for him to enter the machine.

Exodus: Book-wise Deuteronomy mishears. Father states that his sons, Deuteronomy and the noble Exodus, are Masters of the Wheel.

by Oliver Michell

The Mistress: Daily I suck a grey pearl in place of food. Your father Gungulphus swore that Empresses would hand me their treasures, in return for the secret of his wh...wh... *(**The Mistress** stumbles over the word).*

Deuteronomy: *(Encouraging her)* Wh...wh...eeeeel.

Exodus: The ... wh...wh....eeeeel.

The Mistress: The wh... the wh... my mouth cannot tackle its royal title. But now I see that the machine is a shy maiden who will not dance.

Grandma: It shall dance presently, Mistress. Your two fine sons shall feed you all the grey pearls you desire. Gungulphus, my love, do something!

*Hesitating at first, **Gungulphus** begins to unfasten one of the spokes which holds **Mother**'s neck in the Wheel. **Mother** is close to collapse. When released, she falls to her knees but, starving, immediately flings herself towards the plate of Turkish Delight. **Grandma** pulls the plate away as **Mother** crawls towards her, taunting her with it.*

Grandma: The mongrel has its eyes on my roast beef, does it? Back, greedy viper! *(**Mother** collapses).* Now, Gungulphus, angel-child. Show us the dancing for which you were once famous.

*Slowly and reluctantly, **Gungulphus** fits his head into the Wheel and sets about the task of fixing the spoke back into place. **Gungulphus** faces in the opposite direction to **Mother**, i.e. he faces in the same direction as **Exodus** and **Deuteronomy**. **The Mistress** stares straight ahead of her, apparently oblivious to what is happening, until the moment when the spoke is fixed back in place. At this moment she leaps towards the crank and begins* *to turn it violently, spinning* **Deuteronomy**, **Exodus** *and* **Gungulphus** *round. They are clearly in distress.* **Grandma** *shrieks and drops the plate of Turkish Delight.* **Mother** *leaps upon it and lies on the floor, forcing Turkish Delight into her mouth.*

THE END

....

Oliver Michell writes principally for theatre and television. His play *The Tulip Tree* won Best Play at the Oxford University New Writing Festival 2012, judged by Meera Syal, and his play *Philoctetes* was shortlisted for the King's Cross Award 2012. Oliver's short stories are published by SWAMP Writing.

by Oliver Michell

Andy Moseley

Casual Encounters
A Short Play

A suburban house in the stockbroker belt. Lounge, hall and kitchen are visible. **James** *and* **Jennifer** *Rogers (both 38), are in the lounge. They aspire to be pillars of the community and are dressed for a Saturday night's entertaining at home.* **Jennifer** *is looking out of a window.*

Jennifer: Do you think they're coming?

James: Why wouldn't they be?

Jennifer: Maybe they had a better offer.

James: As if there is such a thing.

He gives her an affectionate kiss.

Everything's going to be fine. Don't worry.

Jennifer: Do you think we should have done more food?

James: It's not a dinner party.

Jennifer: I know, but it might be nice to have a proper meal. Don't want them thinking we're stingy.

James: They won't think we're stingy.

Jennifer: How do you know? We've never done this before.

James: No, but the clue is in the name. Wife swapping. Not wife swapping and cheese and wine.

Jennifer: Should I dress up?

James: No, you're fine as you are.

Jennifer: What if they've gone for the glamorous look? I'll look like the booby prize.

James: They won't have dressed up. It's a discreet pastime. They're not going to get out of the car and shout 'hello, we're here for sex.'

Jennifer: I still don't know that we should be doing this.

James: You agreed with the counsellor. She told us we should experiment, do different things.

Jennifer: I think she just meant go to the opera.

James: Well it's too late to change our minds now.

Jennifer: We could go out.

James: We can't. It's bad manners.

Sound of a car pulling up.

Anyway, they're here now.

He goes to the window. A car door opens.

by Andy Moseley

Jennifer: What's she wearing?

James: Nothing much.

Jennifer: What, nothing fancy?

James: No, nothing much. Nothing much at all.

Jennifer: I'll get changed.

Jennifer exits. James answers the door. Peter Morgan (27) and Annette Morgan (25) enter. They look and sound like seasoned swingers.

James tries to appear like he knows what he's doing. Peter's eyes move furtively around the house, as if looking for clues about James and Jennifer's sexual preferences.

James: You found us all right.

Peter: Yeah, not hard really, been round this way a few times with work.

James: Oh right. What do you do?

Peter: I'm in the sales game. Double glazing and all that.

James: I didn't think there was much call for that these days. Thought it was all online.

Peter: They still have to sign the contracts.

James: Right. I'm surprised I haven't seen you around.

Peter: Well you wouldn't. You're a working man, and double glazing is a daytime job. Bit like this one,

	pleasing the lady of the house while the husband's got his hands full.
James:	Yes.
Peter:	So where's the goods?
James:	Pardon?
Peter:	The missus. I mean if I'm doing part-exchange, I want to inspect the merchandise.
James:	She's getting changed.
Peter:	There's no need for her to get dressed up. I mean, it'll be coming off soon enough, eh?
Annette:	Peter, do you have to say that? (*to James*) He's being funny.
James:	So you don't mind that she's getting dressed up?
Peter:	No, it's nice she's making the effort. I just say that so I can find out if it's your first time.
James:	It's not. We've been doing this for ages. I just thought that might be the way round here. We only moved in a month ago.
Peter:	Swinging's swinging mate, wherever it is the rules don't change.
James:	No, course not. Anyway, I'm forgetting my manners. Can I get you a drink?

by Andy Moseley

Peter: That'd be nice. I'll have a bitter.

James: Annette?

Annette: Just a coke for me. I never get drunk when I'm doing it. I like to remember everything.

Peter: Then she can tell me all about it afterwards, can't you?

Annette: Yeah, that's the bit I like best.

James: Right. I'll get the drinks.

Jennifer re-emerges in a black dress.

James: Darling this is Peter and Annette. I'm just going to get them a drink. Can I get you one?

Jennifer: A large glass of wine please.

James goes to the kitchen.

Annette: I was just saying, I prefer not to drink. That way I don't ruin my enjoyment of your husband.

Jennifer: I think a bit of drink heightens the experience. Loosens the inhibitions a bit.

Peter: She don't need her inhibitions loosening. They'd fall apart if they got any looser, wouldn't they babe?

Annette: They would.

Peter: So, do you like what you see?

Jennifer is clearly unsure whether she does.

	I tell you, after you've been with me, you'll never want to swap with anyone again.
Jennifer:	No, I don't think I will.
Annette:	That's the problem. After women have had him they don't want their husbands no more.
Peter:	It's true. There have been a few times when wifey's come round, looking for a bit of extra.
Jennifer:	Oh.
Peter:	I turn them down of course. Wouldn't be fair on Annette. I can't do the wife if she's not getting the husband.
Annette:	He's very considerate like that. A real gentleman.

James returns with a tray and drinks.

James: Sorry it took so long. Can never pour beer without getting a head on it.

They take their drinks.

	Has she been keeping you entertained?
Peter:	Not yet, we normally have a bit of a sit down before the action starts.
James:	No, I meant were you having a nice chat?

Peter:	Oh yes, lovely.
Annette:	Been super, hasn't it Jenny?
Jennifer:	It's Jennifer.
Annette:	Oh sorry. I thought that was just long for Jenny.
Jennifer:	No, Jenny's short for Jennifer.
James:	We've got some food, if you want any?
Annette:	Oh, I'd love some thanks. Can't have sex on an empty stomach. My belly starts rumbling and that's it then.
Jennifer:	We'll bring it in.
Peter:	We'll come with you. Give you a hand.
Jennifer:	That's all right. Bit of a squeeze in there, you stay here and make yourselves at home.

James and *Jennifer* go into the kitchen. Once there, they start talking while putting food onto plates. In the lounge, **Peter** sits, and **Annette** walks around admiring the obvious trappings of wealth.

Jennifer:	I don't want to do it.
James:	Pardon?
Jennifer:	I don't want to do it.
James:	It's too late now. They've come all the way from Godalming.

Casual Encounters

Jennifer: I don't care if they've come from Timbuktu. I don't like them.

James: She's all right.

Jennifer: Oh fine. Sod me. As long as you can shag some twenty-year-old bimbo.

James: She's not twenty.

Jennifer: Not far off it. Why couldn't you get someone our own age?

James: I thought they were.

Jennifer: How? You saw their photos.

James: I thought they were old ones. No one puts new photos on these things. I used the ones of us in Malta.

Jennifer: Malta. That was ten years ago.

James: Eight.

Jennifer: It's still long enough for it to be mis-selling of goods. God, what must they have thought when they saw us?

James: They didn't seem to mind. You should take it as a compliment.

Jennifer: But he looks like a pimp.

James: That's good. Means he knows what he's doing.

by Andy Moseley

Jennifer: It's seedy.

James: Isn't that the point?

Jennifer: Well, yes, but, I don't see why the people have to be seedy too. Why can't they be a bit more, refined?

James: Do it for me darling. Please.

Jennifer: Give me one good reason why.

James: Because if we try and send them home, there's every chance they could cause a scene, and you wouldn't want that, would you?

She quickly weighs the options.

Jennifer: OK. But we're telling them it's our first time.

James: We can't.

Jennifer: We have to. If he thinks I'm a veteran I won't be able to sit down for a week.

Jennifer returns to the lounge before James can answer. He follows behind her with plates.

Jennifer: Here we are.

They put the plates on the coffee table. Annette sits down next to Peter.

Annette: Thanks.

James and Jennifer sit.

Jennifer: This is our first time.

Peter: I knew it.

Jennifer: You did?

Peter: Of course.

James: How?

Peter: You believed everything we said.

Jennifer: So you were making it up?

Peter: Well, I get no complaints about my performance, so you needn't worry about that Jennifer, but I don't get women coming round for extras. Wouldn't get invited back if I did.

James: You go back to places? I never realised. I thought it was just one-offs, casual encounters, not knowing if you might bump into each other again.

Peter: And that little thrill of a guilty secret that only you share?

James: Yes.

Peter: No. It's a hobby. You wouldn't go to a different Zumba class every week, would you?

James: No.

Peter: Exactly.

by Andy Moseley

There is silence as everyone contemplates what to say next.

Annette: It's a very nice house you've got. We're still struggling to get on the property ladder.

Peter: It's hard with the prices.

Annette: I've had some months when I wonder if I should charge for this sort of thing. But that would take the fun out of it.

Jennifer: You don't want to mix business with pleasure.

James: Although you could make a good living if you did.

Annette: Thanks. That's the nicest thing anyone's ever said to me.

Jennifer looks at James. Sandwiches are politely nibbled.

James: So, how do you start these things? Should we finish the sandwiches first?

Jennifer: We could watch a bit of TV and have a game of Scrabble?

Peter and Annette exchange glances. Annette reaches into her handbag.

Annette: We normally start with these.

She produces two sets of handcuffs.

Jennifer: I'm sorry, but we're not doing kinky stuff.

Annette: Don't worry. We're not going to handcuff you while we have our evil way.

James: (*Starting to panic*) You're not police are you? Oh God, please don't arrest us. It's our first time, and we haven't even done it yet.

Jennifer: Darling, they can't arrest us, even if they are police. Wife swapping isn't illegal.

James: So what are the handcuffs for?

Peter: We're going to rob you.

*From inside his trouser pocket **Peter** produces a gun and points it at them.*

What? Aren't you going to say you thought I was just pleased to see you?

Jennifer: I don't believe this.

James: All we wanted was a bit of harmless fun.

Annette: You can have that after we've gone.

James: We can't. You've ruined it now.

Jennifer: Darling, I think we've got more serious things to worry about. We're being held at gunpoint.

James: Why are you doing this to us?

Annette: You're the perfect victims. Posh people who fancy a bit of dirty sex to spice up your marriage. There's loads like you. We do it every weekend.

by Andy Moseley

James: Well you've picked the wrong people today. I'll call the police.

Peter: You won't.

James: I've seen your car. I know the number plate.

Jennifer: James, the man's got a gun.

James: He won't use it. His fingerprints are all over the house.

Jennifer: And now you've reminded him to cover his tracks.

Peter: James, Jennifer, calm yourselves. I'm not going to kill you, and you're not going to call the police. I mean, what would you tell them if you did? There's been no break-in. You invited us in.

Annette: That's the beauty of it. If you tell the police, they'll ask how we came to be here, and once you tell them, you'll be the laughing stock of the station.

Peter: And think of the headlines if they catch us, 'wife swap shame of couple robbed by swingers.' You'd never be able to hold your heads up again.

Annette: You know, you really should be more careful who you let in to your house.

THE END

Andy Moseley grew up in the West Midlands, and did nothing worth wasting 50 words on until he took his first play to Edinburgh. He has since won the 2011 Roy Purdue New Writing Trophy, at the Orange Tree Theatre, Richmond with his play *A Bridge Game Too Far*.

by Andy Moseley

Steve Waters

Interview by Tilly Lunken

Steve Waters's recent theatre plays include *Capernaum in Sixty-Six Books* (Bush Theatre, 2011); *Little Platoons* (Bush Theatre, 2011), adapted for radio and broadcast on BBC Radio 4; *Amphibians*, a site-specific play for Cressida Brown's Offstage Theatre Company (Bridewell Theatre, 2011); *The Contingency Plan* (On the Beach and Resilience, Bush Theatre, 2009), which was shortlisted for the 2009 John Whiting Award and subsequently adapted and broadcast by BBC Radio Drama on Radio 3. For the screen, Steve is currently writing a new version of *The Contingency Plan* (Cowboy Films/Film4).

Steve ran Birmingham University's Master of Philosophy in Playwriting between 2006 and 2011, and currently teaches Creative Writing at UEA on both the Master's and undergraduate Scriptwriting programmes. He is the author of *The Secret Life of Plays* (Nick Hern Books, 2010) and his blog *The Secret Diary of a Playwright* is run weekly by *The Guardian*.

Here, Steve answers questions about his work from Tilly Lunken, a student on the Scriptwriting MA.

In your book *The Secret Life of Plays* you described your process as 'less of a sculptor ... and more akin to a miner'. Can you elaborate on this metaphor?

That comes out of the image that I started the book with, from Beckett, where he said that [he found] it was impossible to speak with any creative authority on writing. And I was exploring why that felt so true; it felt like a very accurate image of what I was in the middle of. I suppose the image of the sculptor is that they stand outside of their material and then they gradually make their work visible, that clichéd image of sculpture, of mastery. Whereas my sense of writing is that you are always lost in the material and [as with a] miner, you are trying to find a way out of it, to get to the outside, then look at it. So I have this feeling of being inside this big envelope with the material with regard to my own writing – which is very different from how I engage with other people's writing. Until I've got it through the draft stage I feel I don't even know what it is.

You write for radio and screen, but predominantly for stage. Are there challenges to writing across these different dramatic forms?

The theatre cannot accommodate every new play that you write (whether the audience are avid for it or not), because of the limitations of the stage and its carrying capacity. I think it is very interesting if, as I have, you adapt from a play to radio, and then ultimately to film, what that reveals about the different media. There is a degree to which if you write for the theatre a lot, you train your imagination, your sense of storytelling, towards constriction and limit, restraint and economy, and sometimes, especially with screenwriting, you have to release this beast which has been stuck in a cage. You have made it enjoy the cage, but now it has to thrive in a completely different context.

There are certain things that you have to let go of. For instance 'real time' doesn't work as well on film or radio because there is something about real time and the immediacy of the actor/audience relationship that is not available to you in the other forms. Actually what I have found is that you embrace these new freedoms but you retain this trained sensibility from theatre, and I think that really good screenwriting has got something of the theatre about it. Certainly really good radio writing has. So yes, they are all very different but they are more related than people seem to imagine.

Do you have a preferred medium in which to write?

I suppose I love the theatre first and foremost. I think again that [this love] is as much about the process of theatre as anything else, it's about working with actors, and it's also about rehearsal – all these things which are much less available to the writer in the other media.

How do you see your academic career fitting alongside your career as a writer? Does the critical theory complement your creative practice?

It's a good question. I am very sceptical about the notion of career. But obviously it is easier to discern a career in academia because it is more stable. I think of myself as being two sorts of person. I have always been a teacher, in schools initially, then in further education, in higher education, now in postgrad education. So there has always been that strand of work and I see that as very intimately linked with my writing. I am probably able therefore to compartmentalise the two activities. There is no doubt that you only have so much imaginative energy, and if you are engaging with other people's writing then focus is pulled away from your own.

Do you find that teaching feeds back into your writing?

Yes, I think it does, although I fear the day when I pick up my own book to see how to approach writing a scene – that would be disastrous! But there's no doubt that sometimes I sit down and think, now why is this project not working out?, or whatever it is, so there is a deeper level of craft to it stemming from academic reflection. If I have a tendency to think that way it is in the latter stages of writing.

You have a reputation for writing work that engages with politics. How important is it for theatre to be engaged with contemporary issues?

If we had a longer time we could have a proper discussion about that. As much as I would like to say it should, I can't bear the phrase 'engaged with contemporary issues', although I know why we use it, because at every level it needs breaking down and rethinking. I often feel I have to get up and defend the right of the theatre to be political but I am also really resistant to what people think that actually might mean in practice.

Is there though a risk in taking on 'State of the Nation' issues; does it perhaps unnecessarily raise the stakes of a play?

Ah, no, I don't think that there is. Although if you brand anything 'State of the Nation' you are quite frankly heading for trouble, because that way of thinking, of responding, is very rhetorical. My imagination is fired up by all sorts of things, but particularly by ideas that manifest themselves in people's lives. Now often those ideas have human implications and so there is within them an urgency that befits the stage as a very urgent medium. I would never say 'must' or 'should' about anything, but I never drift too far away from work that doesn't care about these things at all. It's not so much about politics; it is more about a social engagement, a social texture to the work which is just not negotiable. As soon as it is missing from the work, the work lacks a level of reality, a level of friction and energy.

But do you think that sometimes the popular/critical reception becomes more in focus than the play itself?

People can manipulate your work in that way; I mean it's very appealing for theatres to say, 'Oh we are the first theatre to do it like this', and all those 'about' keywords, so the discussion ends up being about the issues rather than the play. That's unfortunate because you can have an interesting conversation about what a play is about, but it doesn't have any bearing on whether it is a valid theatrical experience. There are so many areas of contemporary experience that are very, very urgent and yet barely understood; those are the things that are extraordinary, as they become secret domains.

Do you see the continuing relevance of such specifically contemporary plays in the future?

Well, if I think of my own work, such as *Little Platoons*, there is no doubt that it is a play for right now. I don't think I would be disappointed if it disappeared into the seas of time because it is an intervention into a very immediate and very local debate [the question of the 'Free Schools' policy]. But most of my other work is not like that at all in that respect, and generally speaking I would baulk at being called journalistic. *The Contingency Plan*, for instance, is a play about families and psychology as much as about climate change. I mean, were we never having to contemplate what climate change might bring us, that play would still hopefully communicate something. But I am suspicious of universality. All great plays go straight into the heart of their times and the fact that we are still interested in them is about other qualities they possess.

New writing is often mistakenly seen as synonymous with young writing; how do you feel about that?

I was rather a late starter as a writer, but I understand that there is something about energy as part and parcel of stage writing, and there is a premium then on finding new young voices. On the other hand, I think we should watch writers grow up and allow them to establish their voices and modify who they are. Surely if you have a powerful play it doesn't matter what age you are; but maybe it is a harder ask

Interview by Tilly Lunken

of a writer of a certain age to engage directly with the contemporary language of the day.

The presumption that somebody is definitely not interesting because of who they are and their age is absolutely ridiculous. But on the other hand, you need to engage with the energy that is coming out of contemporary writing, and there is a risk sometimes of people just writing plays in the abstract. I think that is a mistake, I do think you need to care about what is happening right now, on the stage and in the world. Probably the optimum age for a writer is their 30s, someone who is still young and has a bit of that anger and freshness but has had a bit of experience. I feel the theatre is quite an adult medium and it needs writers who have knocked about a bit.

Do you find a freedom, then, in not being specifically aligned with a generation of playwrights? Of a 'new wave' coming through?

Oh, I just think that's a load of crap. I mean there are waves but they are detected by people in the wake of them. Whose interests does that serve? It is something that people can talk about, get excited about. I certainly think it is fruitful to be surrounded by other writers that you respect and you care about what they are doing, are envious or whatever and are competitive with them. It is possible to say I am a contemporary of David Eldridge, Dennis Kelly, Simon Stephens. Whether other people consider us to be in that group is another matter altogether.

There is something more coherent about the 'In Yer Face' phenomenon because that concerned the wider revival of new writing. But is there anything in common between, say, Joe Penhall and Sarah Kane? They are such different writers from very different positions. So waves? No.

You write of plays as ecosystems; where in the food chain do you see the playwright?

Well, obviously if you think of a play as an ecosystem that is a

Steve Waters

function in itself. If you think of the theatre using the same metaphor clearly the playwright has to be primary because I don't think that you can dispense with the playwright altogether. I can't think of any theatrical movement that has lasted very long without them. So they come at a fairly early point in that food chain. I certainly think that theatres where directors initiate the material rather than writers can soon become quite sterile places, and I say that fully acknowledging the craft of the director in the theatre. But playwrights constantly refresh the possibilities of theatre in a way that is quite difficult for directors to do. The conversation remains within the theatre, whereas the playwright looks out of the theatre to the world and imports new realities into it.

Do you think that this position has changed as your career has progressed?

It comes and goes, I mean you have a bit more clout, but you are only really as powerful as your last utterance. You know, one of the things that interests me is what resources playwrights have to control their own destiny, and I suspect it is both more and less than they imagine. To quote David Eldridge: 'you can always write your way out of trouble'. You can of course write your way into trouble too. So there is some degree to which playwrights can control the conditions of their work. There are one or two that cross over, but I think it is important for creative writers to remain detached from institutions. You get connections – obviously I have a connection with The Bush and with Hampstead Theatre and those are really important. You have really to capitalise on those and play your part in the wider world of the theatre, but also you are a freelancer and there is a degree to which you need to pursue your own trajectory independently.

What is coming up next for you?

Well, what is up next is a radio piece called *The Air Gap*. It's the first original piece I have written for radio in a while and it is an hour's length. It is going to be interesting to see how that one plays as it comes from controversial material: it's about Bradley Manning and his imprisonment. Then I have a piece called *Ignorance* coming out in the autumn at Hampstead Theatre which I am really excited about. It's going to be an interesting year.

....